loose**women**

Girls' Night In

loose**women**
Girls' Night In

Heartfelt advice, inspired innuendo
and toe-curling confessions

HODDER &
STOUGHTON

First published in Great Britain in 2009 by Hodder & Stoughton
An Hachette Livre UK company
Illustrations © Majorie Dumortier

3

Loose Women is an ITV Studios Ltd Production
Copyright © ITV Studios Ltd 2009
Licensed by ITV Global Entertainment

A CIP catalogue record for this title is available from the British Library

Hardback ISBN 978 0 340 91845 6
Trade Paperback ISBN 978 0 340 91858 6

Typeset in ACaslon by Hewer Text UK Ltd, Edinburgh

Printed and bound by Clays Ltd, St Ives plc

Hodder & Stoughton policy is to use papers that are natural,
renewable and recyclable products and made from wood grown in
sustainable forests. The logging and manufacturing processes are expected
to conform to the environmental regulations of the country of origin.

Hodder & Stoughton Ltd
338 Euston Road
London NW1 3BH

www.hodder.co.uk

To Loose Women everywhere

Acknowledgements

We would like to say a big thank you to our talented writer Rebecca Cripps who managed to track us all down and get the secrets out of us!

We would also like to thank the *Loose Women* production team for their support and work behind the scenes on *Girls' Night In* and the show of course; in particular Sue Walton, Donna Gower, Emily Humphries and Karl Newton.

Last but not least, every good book needs a great publisher and we have been very lucky to have had the incredible support and talents of Hodder & Stoughton, in particular our Editor Fenella Bates and her team Damien Frost, Emma Knight, Susan Spratt and Ciara Foley.

CONTENTS

Introduction

Here Come the Girls . . .

Okay, so the fad diet failed, you're never going to be a domestic goddess, the husband's gone AWOL and you've dropped the baby. Does any of it matter when you've got a girls' night in ahead of you? Of course it doesn't! Because we're here to entertain you in the way that only girls know how.

Here's where we'll be sharing the topics that are closest to our hearts. So get ready for toe-curling confessions, saucy tales, eye-popping experiences, pearls of wisdom and celebrity anecdotes – and that's just for starters. We wouldn't forget of course the woeful tales of disastrous relationships, the foolish things the men in our lives get up to, the odd moment of romance, the heartbreak and the heart-racing – a girls' night wouldn't be the same without them, and between us we have *loads* of stories!

From body-image blues and bad-hair days to sex, marriage and dating after divorce, we're telling all right here. Need a friend? Read on for heartfelt advice and inspiring stories that will move and grip you to the core. Need a laugh? Look no further: wait until you hear about what we get up to in the bedroom!

The pros and cons of being single, the highs and lows of long-term love, domestic drudgery, drunken skulduggery, everyday niggles, social dilemmas, tips and secrets . . . it's all here in wickedly funny detail.

So it's time to close the door, put your feet up, pour yourself a glass of something lovely and get stuck in . . .

About Us . . .

As you probably know, we're all very different, which explains why we offer such a wide range of opinions and points-of-view. Here's a little bit of background about each of us.

COLEEN NOLAN

Witty, outspoken Coleen Nolan is the queen of sidesplitting one-liners. Whether she's flirting with gorgeous male guests or complaining about the hubby, her saucy humour and sense of comic timing regularly reduce the *Loose Women* panel to helpless giggles. She also loves to get stuck into a serious discussion and is known for her forthright, often controversial, opinions.

Although she jokes about the travails of married life, Coleen loves being a wife and mother. She married musician Ray Fensome in November 2007 after he proposed to her on her 40th birthday. The couple have one daughter, Ciara, who was born in June 2001. Coleen was previously married to actor Shane Richie and they have two sons, Shane Jnr and Jake. After ten years of marriage, their divorce was finalised in 1999.

Coleen is a member of the celebrated Nolan Sisters, whose legendary success included chalking up two Royal Performances, phenomenal record sales in Britain and more than 15 million records sold worldwide. She has a weekly column in *Woman* magazine and a parenting column in the *Daily Mirror*. She has just written her autobiography *Upfront & Personal*.

CAROL MCGIFFIN

Totally upfront and honest, Carol McGiffin says what no one else dares to say (but wishes they could!). Never one to follow the crowd, she is often the lone voice of dissent at the centre of a controversial discussion. Respected and admired for her no-holds-barred openness, she tells it like it is and doesn't pull her punches.

Carol also *does* what no one else dares to. She was snapped flashing her lacy knickers at the Royal Television Awards 2008 and caused a stir after appearing to strip on *Loose Women* to celebrate National Nude Day (the wonders of tv!)

Famously candid about her sex life, or lack thereof, she admitted many times on the show that she hadn't had any action for quite a while! But that all changed when she met her 'gorgeous boyfriend' at the *Loose Women* wrap party before their 2008 summer break.

Carol's relationship has definitely given her a glow. However, she did genuinely enjoy being single, and who can blame her? A self-confessed serial snogger, in her singleton days she kissed Russell Brand, Gary Rhodes and Danny Dyer on air, and countless random strangers on wild nights out.

Interestingly, the flipside of Carol the party girl is a true romantic – she holds marriage sacred and believes in 'the one'.

But freedom remains hugely alluring. An adventurous traveller, she likes nothing better than to pop over to Thailand for a long weekend, and she knows Paris and New York like the back of her hand.

Carol is a natural on TV, but her roots are in radio; she started her broadcasting career as co-host of the now legendary Chris Evans shows on GLR. Their partnership developed off air as well, they married in 1991 but separated three years later. Other radio work has included the award-winning Talk Radio breakfast show alongside Paul Ross. She also presented a Sunday morning show for LBC, but left the station in February 2008.

JANE MCDONALD

Hugely popular singer Jane McDonald has brought sparkle to *Loose Women* since 2004. In Jane, down-to-earth charm meets stylish chic. Her common sense and thoughtful, heartfelt advice combined with quick wit have made her very popular with viewers.

Jane's a superstar diva who never forgets she's a miner's daughter and a girl-next-door. The grounded girl in sky-high heels remains proud of her Wakefield roots. When she's not touring with her band or staying over in London to appear on *Loose Women*, she can be found at home in her hometown with her beloved mum, who makes a mean shepherd's pie.

After toughing out her early career on the Northern club circuit, sultry Jane became an overnight celebrity on BBC docusoap, *The Cruise*. Around 14 million viewers watched her romance with manager Henrik Brixen unfold on the show. The couple tied the knot in a televised ceremony in 1998, but have since divorced.

Jane's popularity with audiences on *The Cruise* led to presenting work on BBC's *National Lottery* and ITV's *Star for a Night*. She released her eighth album in August 2008, the same month that she appeared on *Return of the Cruise* to celebrate the show's 10th anniversary. The album reached No 7 in the charts and she continues to pack out venues nationwide.

Like Carol, Jane always said that she was happy to remain single; now, like Carol, she is glowing with happiness after teaming up with her former childhood sweetheart, Ed Rothe. However, unlike Carol, her favourite indulgence still appears to be a lovely cup of tea!

SHERRIE HEWSON

Ever-so-slightly-eccentric actress Sherrie Hewson isn't afraid to reveal her foibles, but did you know that she can't stand to be anywhere near a walnut? That's right, a walnut. Sherrie's unique take on life has made her a favourite with the *Loose Women* audience since 2003. Her quirky outlook, vivid imagination and self-deprecating sense of humour ensure that there's never a dull moment when she's on the panel.

Born into a showbiz family, talented Sherrie began performing on stage at the age of four. She spent her childhood touring the UK in revues but it's her talent as an actress that has made her famous and at fifteen she won the prestigious Olivier Award for Best Newcomer and went on to study at RADA.

Her varied television and film career took off in the 1970s and she appeared in *In Loving Memory* with Thora Hird, *Home to Roost* with John Thaw, *Love for Lydia* with Jeremy Irons and

Russ Abbot's *Madhouse*. Her role as accident-prone Maureen in *Coronation Street* launched her career as a soap star in 1993, when audiences were instantly won over by her portrayal of the ditzy shop assistant. Her comedy partnership with on-screen husband Reg Holdsworth went on to become one of the soap's most popular double acts. Sherrie waved goodbye to Weatherfield in 1997 (although she has popped back since), and later played major roles in the ITV1 soaps *Crossroads* and *Emmerdale*. Her film credits include *The Slipper and the Rose* with Richard Chamberlain and *Hanover Street* with Harrison Ford.

In March 2008, bookworm Sherrie revealed a hidden crime-writing talent, after winning BBC show *Murder Most Famous*. Her novel is being published as part of Pan Macmillan's 'quick reads' in celebration of World Book Day 2009.

In 2004 Sherrie and her husband of twenty-five years Ken Boyd separated. Sherrie has a daughter Keeley and baby grandson Oliver, both of whom she adores.

LYNDA BELLINGHAM

Lynda Bellingham's no-nonsense views and good-natured grumpiness made her an instant hit with viewers when she joined *Loose Women* in 2007. She is also much loved for her warmth, honesty and intuitive intelligence. Lynda believes that women over 50 are ignored by society, but she's not about to put up and shut up! A darling of the stage and screen.

Lynda's TV career spans from the early 70s when she appeared in the first daytime soap *General Hospital*. During the 80s she appeared in the long running Oxo campaign which made her a much-loved face of the nation. This led to roles in several

TV series, including Helen Herriot in *All Creatures Great and Small*, the title role in *Faith in the Future* and appearances in *At Home with the Braithwaites* and *Bonkers*. In 2004, she played against type when she took the role of recurring villainess Irene Radford in *The Bill*.

In October 2007, Lynda received glowing reviews for her acclaimed role in *Vincent River* in London's West End. In autumn 2008 she starred in the critically acclaimed stage version of *Calendar Girls*, happily taking her husband on tour with her throughout the UK. She has two sons named Michael and Robbie and her mothering instinct is often seen on the show.

On 31 May 2008 Lynda married Michael Pattermore (aka Mr Spain) who she met in Spain in 2004.

DENISE WELCH

Funny, frank and endearingly honest, Denise Welch is always willing to reveal her own experiences, however personal! Whatever the topic, from plastic surgery to infidelity, she opens up without hesitation. That's why everyone loves Denise. Plus, she's a really good laugh.

Since joining *Loose Women* in 2005, Denise has confessed to a need to be whistled at by builders and admitted her love of wild all-nighters. She has talked frankly about why she underwent eye surgery for cosmetic reasons and spoken honestly about her battles with depression and drinking. She's not averse to dishing the dirt on actor husband Tim Healy's hilarious bad habits, either.

Currently starring as flirtatious French teacher Steph Haydock in BBC drama *Waterloo Road*, Denise was already a well-established actress before she joined the cast in 2006. Her television break came in 1986 in ITV's hit drama *Spender* and she also appeared in *Auf Wiedersehen, Pet,* where she starred alongside Tim Healy, before they were married. They were recently reunited on screen again when Tim appeared as her love interest in *Waterloo Road.*

Denise became a household name in 1993 when she played saucy seductress Marsha Stubbs in ITV's *Soldier, Soldier.* She joined *Coronation Street* in 1997 as Rovers Return barmaid Natalie Horrocks and her vampish character soon began an affair with Sally Webster's husband Kevin. Who could forget the classic moment when Sally slapped Natalie across the face when she discovered what the pair were up to?

Denise and Tim have two sons, Matthew and Louis. Last year they celebrated 20 years of marriage. There wasn't a dry eye in the studio when Tim made a guest appearance on the show on Valentine's Day 2008 and serenaded Denise with 'Have I Told You Lately?'

JACKIE BRAMBLES

Jackie Brambles has been a broadcast journalist for 23 years and is one of the two main anchors on *Loose Women.* Calm and unflappable, with a wry sense of humour, Jackie is ideally suited to the job of cooling things down when panellists or guests start overheating.

Jackie began her broadcasting career in radio aged 19 at her local radio station in Scotland. After a year of presenting the Evening Show for Capital Radio in London, she joined BBC Radio 1 as the first ever female primetime presenter, going on to double audiences on the Lunchtime show from two to four million listeners.

She relocated to the USA in 1994, where she initially worked as a contributor to BBC Radio before moving into the American media. She joined CBS as the Morning News Anchor for radio and as the Weekend News Anchor for the TV News in San Francisco, where she lived for over five years. During the initial boom years of Silicon Valley, Jackie also worked as a media consultant for Intel, Sony and Oracle. In 1999, Jackie moved south to Los Angeles and joined the LA Bureau for GMTV as Foreign Correspondent.

During her six years in Hollywood, Jackie interviewed the world's most famous stars multiple times and covered a vast variety of news events, ranging from the Oscars to 9/11. In 2005 she returned to Britain and continued working for GMTV in London for a year.

In fact the year of 2005 was pivotal for Jackie. Starting with her return to the UK after eleven years away, she married family friend David Tod and became pregnant with their first baby. She left GMTV in 2006 following the birth of her son Stanley and the discovery that she was again expecting! Jackie was invited to join *Loose Women* temporarily whilst pregnant and shortly after giving birth to her daughter Florence, became a permanent member of the *Loose Women* team.

ANDREA MCLEAN

Keeping the ladies in check is the show's other main anchor Andrea McLean, whose gentle warmth and charm always ensure that peace prevails, even when she vehemently disagrees with what is being said. Andrea joined the panel at the beginning of 2007 and has been a regular on the show ever since.

Andrea trained as a journalist and graduated with a BA Hons in Modern Studies at Coventry University. She then set off around the world with a backpack, taking on jobs as diverse as a grill chef, barmaid, shop assistant, receptionist and factory worker. On her return in 1993, she gained her Post Graduate Certificate in Periodical Journalism and started her career as a travel writer.

When Andrea joined *Loose Women* she was already a familiar television face, best known for presenting the weather on *GMTV*. In July 2008, Andrea announced she was leaving the early-morning breakfast show after eleven years of four a.m. starts, so she can at last have the occasional weekday lie-in!

In January 2006, Andrea took part in ITV1's reality ice-skating competition *Dancing on Ice*. After being eliminated in week three along with fellow ex-contestant Andi Peters, she and Andi went on to present the weekday show *Dancing on Ice Extra* for the rest of the show's run. Andrea has also presented *Our House* for UKTV Style.

Scottish-born Andrea was raised in Trinidad and Tobago, hence her distinctive Scots/Caribbean accent. She moved back to the UK when she was 15 and now lives in Surrey with her partner Steve, and her two children Finlay and Amy.

Chapter 1

That's What Friends Are For

From brand new bosom buddies to childhood pals, best mates and party partners, where would we be without our friends? Bored and lonely, with no one to gossip or moan to, that's where!

Loose Women is really all about friendship and how friends can get you through the tough times and bring mischief and joy to your life.

Whether you want a laugh, a cry, or a good long chat, whether you go out, stay in or spend hours on the phone, whether you keep in touch by text, calling, email or Facebook, friends are the backbone of everyone's lives. And we wouldn't have it any other way.

GIRLFRIENDS

JACKIE: No matter how great your relationship is, or how well you get on with your partner, your life is poorer for the lack of good women friends and family. The way women talk to each other and relate to one another is unique, and most women feel that other women are crucial in their lives, whether it's Mum, a sister or a best friend (and not forgetting your gay friends, of course!).

COLEEN: With me, it's my sisters, although I've got lots of great women friends as well. Not to mention you bunch of nutters.

CAROL: We love you too, Coleen!

JACKIE: My friends are scattered around the globe, so to come to London once a week to have a couple of days with the girls at *Loose Women* is just fantastic for me. It's a ready-made group of girlfriends.

The nature of the show is such that we all do a lot of talking about our lives. There's quite a lot of trust involved in doing that, because obviously there are things said in meetings that aren't always said on the screen. We know a lot about each other and we trust each other.

Then the girls and I sometimes go out for a drink after we've done a show, which is really nice. We all stay at the same hotel, so we'll have a couple of glasses of wine and a bite to eat.

CHILDHOOD FRIENDS

ANDREA: My best friend is a girl called Jane. I have one sister and Jane is like another sister to me. She's probably the only person I can tell everything to, although sometimes I spare her because I think, Oh god, she must be bored of me!

Jane and I were christened together in Trinidad and she

was my birth partner when I had Amy, whose middle name is Jane. I was frightened that Steve, man that he is, might not be able to cope, so I asked if I could have two people in there when Amy was born, and they relented.

COLEEN: I stay in touch with one girl I went to school with. It's great because we might not speak for six months or a year, and then we'll get on the phone and it's like we're back at school. Although we don't speak as regularly as I'd like, if I was having a party, she would be first on the list.

DENISE: I don't see a lot of my old grammar school friends because we all live all over the place. But we have all stayed in touch, mainly because my dad, bless him, has made sure that we've all got each others' numbers.

JACKIE: My friends are spread out all over the place, in San Francisco, Los Angeles and London. I'm still in touch with a couple of childhood friends, but I don't get to see them much. Fortunately, the great thing about old friends is that sometimes you only see them once in a while, but it's just like you saw them yesterday.

DENISE: My best girlfriend Rose and I met when I was eighteen and she was seventeen. We went to drama school together. Two and a half years ago, Rose moved from London up north and now we live much closer together, but our lives are so mad that I think I saw as much of her when she lived in blooming London.

It's amazing how the time passes. One minute you're teenagers and the next you're fifty. My ex-boyfriend is a teacher and the other day he said to me, 'You know, Den, I've been teaching for thirty years.'

'Don't be so ridiculous!' I said, and then I thought, Oh god, he has! Yet he's still Rob Taylor that I used to fancy coming out of biology at school. That's my enduring mental picture of him.

My sister is forty-seven, but when she talks about people she was at school with, they're still about nine in my mind, when in fact they're also forty-seven now! To me, her friend Deb is still Deborah Such-and-Such who used to ride along on her little pony. It's just ridiculous. I've got to start accepting the passing of time.

JANE: Look in the mirror, love. That's the biggest shock of all!

FRIENDS OF ALL AGES

CAROL: Most of my friends of my age are in couples. They're married or they've got kids. So it's lucky I enjoy going out with couples, because I don't know as many single people any more.

When you're single, you need to find other single people to go out with, so I've found that my girlfriends are getting younger. Some of my girlfriends are as young as twenty-three, my niece's age! We always have a great time, because we go out and have fun.

DENISE: I love socialising with the youngsters. Age isn't an issue for me. My oldest son Matthew's friends are brilliant and sometimes he'll come out with my friends and me, because half of my friends are not much older than he is. One of the great things about this industry is that it's full of young people. At the other end of the scale, my parents have always had friends of all ages, younger and older, and I'm friendly with some of their friends. I feel lucky to have such a huge network of people from different parts of my life.

CATCHING UP

SHERRIE: Paul O'Grady is one of my oldest friends, but we never seem to have time to catch up, because we both work like insane people. So it was great to see him again for the Pride of Britain Awards last year, even if we did get wet and cold standing out on Westminster Bridge for hours waiting for the links to television, before walking five miles through the back streets of London in the rain! We missed the show and the awards too, but it was fine, because it was for breast cancer, and anything for breast cancer has got to be worth it. There but for the grace of god go all of us.

We walked down all those little roads behind Tower Bridge. I have lived in London since 1969 and I remember those backs streets before they were posh, when the area was really old London, very *Oliver*. Paul even showed me the steps where Nancy was killed by Bill Sikes.

How pretty old London still is! Paul showed me the old Vauxhall Tavern where he used to do Lily and a little old Victorian house where he used to have parties all night. The little Mudlark pub is still there and it remains very atmospheric.

Back in 1969, we would never have walked around that area at night, because it was dire – all the way down to the docks. You'd see dead dogs on the road and people not caring. But it's all posh these days. All those dark, dingy flats that you would never have even considered buying now cost the earth.

It was wonderful catching up on news about our friends, families and old times as we wandered around. We've known each other fifteen years and whenever we see each other we talk about a particular time we worked together in a pantomime, when we had the most outrageous, hysterical six weeks of our lives.

It is lovely to have Paul as a friend, because he is a true friend, one of the kindest, most giving men you'd ever meet in your life. His kind nature shone out in the way he treated our friend Reg, who did a drag act called Regina Thong. Reg was my oldest friend in the world and Paul's as well, although we didn't know it at the time.

When Reg contracted cancer and couldn't work, Paul looked after him and cared for him in every single way until the day he died. He is a very special person.

COLEEN: Aah! That's so lovely.

JANE: Warms the cockles, it does. That's what friends are for, as they say. Count your blessings, love, you've got a great friend there.

WHO DO YOU TURN TO?

ANDREA: In a crisis I'll turn to Steve, first of all. But every couple has times when they're fed up with each other and then I talk to my friend Jane about it, or the girls. We normally come in on a Monday and say, 'Aargh. He's driving me mad!'

For me, being on this show has been like therapy, because I'm a very private person and I don't necessarily even talk to my friends about some of the things we talk about.

When I first started, I felt quite uncomfortable with some of the topics. I'd say, 'I'll host this bit as I don't really want

17

to give my opinion,' and they would let me steer around it. However, listening to the girls' stories has made me question why on earth I thought I was the only one who went through this or that. We've all had tricky times.

You tentatively mention something in a meeting and get slammed down. 'That's nothing! Look what happened to me.'

It makes you think, God, you're right. What am I doing?

So now I've opened up massively and come to terms with so many things that I'd built up in my head to be a big deal.

LYNDA: I now turn to Michael in a crisis, but for many years it was my parents that I turned to. Losing my parents was a defining moment. I lost them within a month of each other. My mother had Alzheimer's, so I'd lost her two or three years before. Dad was fine, but then Dad died just after Christmas 2005 and Mum died a month later.

I'd just started my relationship with Michael, which was a blessing, but also confusing. I actually broke it off with him around that time; I felt that I was engaging with him because of the death of my parents and didn't see him for two or three weeks. But, brilliantly, he persevered with me. He wasn't put off – and he could easily have been put off. Instead he was there for me and let me work my way through it.

JANE: My mother has never let me down, in any shape or form. She's my best friend, my confidante and I would always turn to her in a crisis. I can tell her absolutely anything, which is another thing that really shocks everybody. I have a brilliant relationship with her: no matter what's on my mind, I can talk to her about it. My grandmother was the same. She was really, really broad-minded, so I think it's a characteristic of the matriarchs in the family.

CAROL: I wouldn't like to burden my family with my problems. They've got their own problems. Of course, if I was in trouble they'd do anything to help me out, but I would probably go to my friends first. I've got a couple of good girlfriends who I've known for years and don't live too far away.

COLEEN: And you've got us, of course! What would you do without us?

CAROL: Oh yes, I was forgetting! I must have been on the show too long . . .

GAY BEST FRIEND

CAROL: My best friends in the world are a gay couple. I go on holiday with them all the time. We joke that there are three of us in the relationship, because every time they go on holiday, I'm there, in the middle, interfering! I'm like their adopted sister.

    A lot of my friends are gay. It makes sense to hang around with gay men if you're single, because they're the same as you. They haven't got kids and as a result have money to spend.

DENISE: I just love my gay friends. They make me laugh more than anybody. I think that gay people have to develop a sense of humour just to get through, even though homosexuality is much more accepted now. Apart from sense of humour,

 there's nothing very different about them. My gay friends are very loyal, but all my friends are loyal. Perhaps they adore me in a different way, though. That's not a vanity thing: they just cherish me a bit more, my gay friends.

I love their stories about their sex lives and I love hearing about these places that they go to. It's fascinating. Tim is great with them and they're fabulous with Louis, my youngest. Of course they all love Matt, my eldest, because he's gorgeous!

One of my best gay friends writes for one of the national newspapers. He could put me in tabloid jail and never does. I love his sense of humour. When someone introduces a new boyfriend to him, he says things like, 'Did you tell Neil about the eighteen men you shagged after that dinner party that night? You didn't? Oh, I thought you would have told him!'

I very rarely fall out with friends, as I tend to bottle up problems and just hope they will go away with time. Yet I've fallen out with my journalist friend countless times. Then again, although I've fallen out with him probably more than with any other friend, I can't not have him in my life.

Stephen is my other long-standing gay friend. I've known Stephen since 1984, when we lived in Brighton. Then there are Nick and Paul, who I met around eight years ago at Mr Gay UK. I just love their company.

JACKIE: One of my best friends is a gay man called Michael. It's a unique relationship. It's fun and it's honest. It's a bit like being friends with a woman in a good-looking man's body.

Michael knows where all the skeletons are! Unfortunately

he's in Los Angeles, but we're still in regular touch. We've been friends for years and years and will be forever.

LOSING AND DROPPING FRIENDS

ANDREA: I've dropped friends and I've been dropped. Being dropped is really hurtful. When it happened to me, I didn't understand what I had done and I still don't understand. The people in question were a couple I'd known since I was eighteen. I wasn't the only one they suddenly stopped talking to though. They had been through some fairly rough times as a couple and perhaps they wanted a fresh start.

JACKIE: I dropped a couple of friends in America. They turned out to be a little bit too wacky and bizarre, so I gradually cut off contact. People in LA tend to be very transitory and it's all quite superficial, so I was extraordinarily lucky to make three fantastically close, lifelong friends there. I had lots of other friends and acquaintances and a good social circle, but I made these very good friendships too, which is fairly rare because it's a bit of a bonkers place and attracts quite a lot of bonkers people.

LYNDA: I'm very loyal, but if that loyalty is broken, that's it. Someone would have to do something very grim to me for that to be the case, though.

ANDREA: Yes, because you're very tolerant, Lynda. Dropping friends is the hardest thing, I find, not that I've had to do it much, luckily. I'm no good at gradually losing contact, like you are, Jackie. I'm the kind of person who will keep on meeting up with people even though I really don't want to see them any more. I'm just too polite.

I'd rather fudge the issue and say, 'I'm quite busy at the moment,' or 'I'll get back to you,' and hope that it will drift long enough that eventually it just won't happen. But I did drop a friend once. I was really bad at it because I'd never done it before.

Why is it that the person you want to drop is really insistent and doesn't get the hint? One person kept on and on at me, and so we kept meeting up, even though she should have been able to tell that I didn't really want to.

One day at GMTV I was standing at the mirror, fixing my makeup, and I said to a friend, 'Oh god, I've got another lunch with this girl.'

She said, 'Why don't you cancel it?'

'I can't, because, you know . . .' I said.

'You're prepared to give up two hours of your life to spend with someone that you'd rather not?' she said. 'Make it easy for yourself and say, "It's been really lovely, but can we cool it for a little bit?" and just leave it.'

Instead, I did the most cowardly thing you can do. I stood her up. I've felt rotten about it ever since.

It was before the days of mobiles, so I was at home, looking at my clock, thinking, She'll be there. It wasn't even like it was a group of us. It was just the two of us meeting.

Later that afternoon my phone rang. It was her. I didn't answer it. 'I must have got the date wrong,' she said on the answerphone. 'I'm really sorry. Do you want to ring me and we'll rearrange?'

I didn't ring her back. Finally, she left another message

saying, 'Okay, I get it now. You obviously don't want to see me. I can't believe you did that to me. You could have just told me to my face!' Then she hung up.

I still feel bad about it because she's right. It was a really horrible way to do it and I was a coward. But if I hadn't done it that way, I would probably still be going to see her now, saying, 'This is lovely but I've got to rush off now.'

CAROL: Cor, you must really hate confrontation, Andrea!

ANDREA: I do hate it! I can't bear it!

CAROL: You were so over-polite that you inevitably ended up being really rude! That's going from one extreme to another, isn't it? I can understand why you did it, but I would have just said to her, 'Don't you get the hint? Can't you sense that I'm always avoiding your calls?'

ANDREA: I know that now! I'd never do anything like it again. In fact, the whole experience taught me to be a lot more upfront about things.

JANE: You learn from your mistakes, don't you, love? I'm a little bit more guarded than I was when I first came into this business, many years ago. Back then I was so naïve and green that I trusted everybody. I thought that the things they did on my behalf must be in my interests. But you get your fingers burnt along the way so many times that, in the end, you think, It's not going to happen again! There are only so many times that you can get burnt before you realise, Now this must be something to do with me.

In a way, I'm really glad that I experienced it, although it's still hard to believe that people will try and pull the wool over your eyes and tell you things that are completely untrue, simply for their own gain.

I am more wary now, because it's a hard business we're in. I don't have an awful lot of friends and my work colleagues are very much my closest friends. I have a very close-knit circle around me all the time. It's like a big protective metal ring around me. As long as I've got that protection, I can remain the same naïve, down-to-earth Yorkshire lass that everybody saw on *The Cruise* ten years ago.

LYNDA: It's interesting you say that, Jane. My sons and Michael say that I'm an easy target and that people have taken me for a ride. I would argue that maybe that was true a couple of times in my life, but who hasn't been taken for a ride? In the main, I haven't suffered at the hands of others, really. Maybe that's because I have chosen not to notice it, or because I've chosen to move on. I move very fast and I either take people with me or they get left behind if they don't keep up. I certainly don't suffer fools gladly.

I've found that women aren't always helpful to each other, although a group of really good women can show you that it's possible to have a lot of fun within your parameters, if you give yourself a break and don't compare yourself to anyone.

The thing is, competitiveness can be very destructive among women. When people are younger, it's: 'Is your child brighter than my child? Does your child sleep better than my child?' So when they get to their fifties, what are they going to compare? 'Are your wrinkles less visible than mine?'

I say to them, 'Calm down, Mr Mainwaring, and relax! Enjoy yourself, especially if you've got your health.' If you get through your fifties and sixties without succumbing to cancer, then you're going to have another fifteen or twenty years, if you're lucky. You've got to be positive about it. Otherwise, why bother?

I know that bad things happen to people – and indeed they've happened to me on several occasions – but I truly believe that if you try to make a plan and achieve certain goals, good things are more likely to happen to you. You might get waylaid in certain areas along the way – you might go sideways instead of forwards, but you'll feel better in your head if you have a mission, and that will translate to your body and life in general. Good women friends can definitely help you get there.

JACKIE: They certainly can. We're proof of that, aren't we?

FRIENDS WITH AN EX

LYNDA: My first husband and I are friends now. I didn't speak to or see him for twenty-odd years, but when I was in Russia and my divorce with my second husband went through, I had a whole load of time to think about my life. I realised that my first husband and I had a lot in common and would always have been good friends if we hadn't got married, so it seemed daft not to have the friendship now.

KEEPING IN TOUCH – HOW?

ANDREA: I've got a really dear friend up in Chester who is a schoolteacher; we met working in a bar when I was nineteen. We don't see each other that much because we both work, she's got three kids and I've got two, but we're on the phone all the time.

JACKIE: My Monday nights when I'm in London are when I get to do my socialising. That's also when I make my long-distance phone calls to America, because I know I'll have lots of peace and quiet to have a grown-up conversation. But sometimes I use my Monday night as an opportunity to catch up on sleep. Most of the time – at the moment – my husband and I are quite chronically sleep deprived, so a whole night's sleep is a treat.

I don't tend to talk to the outside world when I'm at home, because it's just impossible! I do quite a lot of texting, though.

COLEEN: I'm very much a text freak, I much prefer to text than talk on the phone. When I come off set, I always check my phone to see if there's a text. It doesn't matter what a text says, I just get excited when I see I've got one. I also love writing letters and cards. For me, emails just aren't the same as writing a letter.

I hate talking on the phone, probably because my job is to talk constantly, but I'll text all day. I get into trouble for not calling people. My friends say, 'I can't believe you didn't call me when I texted you!'

The thing is, I'm away quite a lot. So when I get home I want to be with Ciara and the boys, if they're there. I certainly don't want to get in and say, 'Hi Ciara,' and then spend an hour on the phone. So sometimes I text people back and say, 'I'm busy right now. I'll call when I can.' It's a lie, but not a bad one.

SHERRIE: I've got a wonderful friend called Anne, who's a life coach. Yesterday, out of the blue, she texted me. 'Hello lovely lady, thinking of you,' the text went. 'Know that you bring such colour to this world, so carry on showing people that colour, because it gives great joy,' it went on. It is so heartening to know that someone thinks that about me. It made me think to myself, For god's sake get on with life and stop worrying!

CAROL: I know everyone is really busy, but friends should look out for single people living on their own, and single people should look out for each other. All they need to do is phone them up. It worries me sometimes living on my own, because I've always had this fear of dying alone in my flat and no one caring. I hate the thought of someone finding me dead on the floor covered in flies three weeks later!

JANE: Oh what a cheery thought! But I take your point. Only, Carol, believe me love, there are no flies on you now, and there never will be.

DENISE: But perhaps you'd better move in with your bloke, just to make sure! Oh yes, that'll be next, won't it? A traditional, white, blooming McGiffin wedding!

SOCIAL NETWORKING

ANDREA: A lot of my friends are on Facebook, and they keep saying, 'You must join!' but I can't be bothered. If I want to speak to someone, I'll speak to them – or text or email them.

JACKIE: I'm a dinosaur when it comes to social networking sites. I've never been on Facebook in my life and I'm not vaguely interested in it. It's probably my age – it's a young single person's thing – but I think it's weird and a bit scary to want the world to know what's going on in your life. Coming from someone who works in telly that might sound a bit strange, but TV is my job and then I go home and live my normal private life.

I don't even know the Facebook terminology. It just makes no sense to me that everybody wants to spend hours saying hello to each other online and trying to accumulate three thousand friends, people they've never met.

DENISE: The makeup girls put me on Facebook and I enjoy it. It's quite useful too, because I never remember people's email addresses, so I mainly use Facebook to send messages. It's quite nice to get the odd personal friend request, too, especially if it's someone from the past. You immediately want to go onto their profile and see what they look like these days. But I don't obsess with it at all. I can't be bothered with it. You get a message saying, 'So-and-so has written on your wall', but I don't really know where my wall is, so I don't follow it up.

I dread the words, 'Rhys has tagged you in a photo on

Facebook', because you can guarantee it will be a picture of me with a glass of wine and fag in hand. Oh god!! There's nothing you can do about that. So wherever you go where someone says, 'Can I have a photo with you?' more often than not they just put you on Facebook. Oh my god! People have lost jobs because of that! All it takes is for their boss to see them on a night out, wide-eyed and obviously partying heavily. Nightmare!

Chapter 2

Looking Good

If you believe the surveys, twenty per cent of us are on diets at any one time, fifty per cent of us would consider having cosmetic surgery and ten per cent actually hate what we look like. What's that all about, then?

Here's where we discuss the way we look and how we feel about our looks, including our attitudes to weight, hair, makeup and ageing. As you'll see, we may not be entirely happy with nature's gifts, but we're determined to make the best of what we've got, with or without a little extra help!

ATTITUDES TO FOOD/WEIGHT & DIETS

COLEEN: Since I've lost weight, friends and family members I haven't seen in a while tend to say, 'My god!' when they see me.

There's also quite a lot of recognition from the general public. People often say, 'You look so much fatter on the telly!'

Oh, thanks! Still, I suppose it's better than the other way round.

DENISE: Tell me about it! If I had a pound for every time someone said, 'Ooh, you're much prettier in the flesh', I'd be a rich woman. The television obviously makes me look like I'm a complete munter.

COLEEN: I've always had weight issues, really. I'm prone to putting it on very quickly – although, luckily, I can lose it as well. I think when I was bigger I tended to play the happy fat girl in the middle, full of self-deprecating jokes. I played that role for a long time.

I was cool about it, though. Now people say, 'So you were really unhappy behind the scenes, then?' But I wasn't unhappy. I definitely didn't go home and have major crying fits. It's just that I feel better and more confident in myself now. I feel sexier, so therefore I'm just more confident.

I've met big people who I think are really attractive, just because they are so vivacious and full of life that you see past their appearance. You can have a woman with the most beautiful face and body in the world, but if she hasn't got anything to say, it's boring. Once you've initially thought, Wow!, unless the whole package is there, it's very dull.

JACKIE: I've struggled with my weight on and off over the years, but I'm probably the thinnest I've ever been now. Having two kids in quick succession means that you don't have time to eat and you're permanently on the go. That's my keep-fit tip!

DENISE: I've never been weight-obsessed like some people are in this industry, but I'm struggling now because for twenty years my weight was controlled by my illness. In the past, when I put on a bit of weight, I would undoubtedly hit a slump and lose half a stone. I lost at least half a stone every time I had a depressed episode, because I literally cannot eat anything when I'm ill. I just can't do it.

Now my illness is no longer ruling my life, I really struggle because I love my food and it's boring to have to watch what you eat. I'm not obsessive, though. I'd love to be a size ten again and I still get into some size ten clothes, but really I'm a size twelve and I'm happy with that.

Of course, women will always want to be half a stone lighter. You want people to say, 'Don't lose any more weight!' and, 'You look ill!' It's so silly, especially as I'm a character actress on TV and I shouldn't be bothered about people going, 'Phoar, look at her!' I always look crap on telly anyway.

Last Christmas, I was the heaviest I've ever been. I went on a cruise and I felt like I would have eaten small children if they'd come past me. There was a twenty-four-hour buffet and I spent about twenty-three hours in it a day – and all because I knew that a women's magazine was going to help me to go on a diet when I came back. It was almost like it gave me an excuse.

COLEEN: My attitude to food has definitely changed as I've lost weight. Obviously, the food I'm eating is a lot healthier now and I've finally grasped that the more you put in the fatter you are going to get. Now I try to eat less more often rather than binge. If I have a cup of tea and I want a chocolate biscuit, I'll have a chocolate biscuit. But I won't have the packet of chocolate biscuits that I used to have before.

It's a combination of willpower and habit, I think. Once you get into the habit of having one biscuit instead of the packet, you don't feel you need the packet any more. Mentally, I'm all right with one biscuit these days.

ANDREA: I must admit that feeling big was quite an issue for me. I'm really relieved that I've lost my baby weight. Now, when I'm dressed up for a do, I look at myself and think, Hang on, I'm all right! Obviously I see the bits that I don't like as well, but overall it's not bad.

DENISE: I don't like to stand naked and look at myself in the mirror and I never have. I prefer myself with clothes on. I try to have a spray tan and keep it up, so that when I do catch a glimpse of myself in the Debenhams changing room, I don't just want to kill myself! Those moments are never very nice, but I'm really not hung up about it.

MAKEUP

JACKIE: I only wear a lot of makeup when I'm at work. I don't wear much at home, at all. I certainly don't have as many pots and potions as Jane. When you go into Jane's dressing room, it's like walking into Selfridges department store. She's got several wardrobe options, nine pairs of shoes and eighteen lip glosses laid out immaculately. Everywhere she goes, it's the same. But all my stuff is crammed into one little bag.

JANE: One bag? Oh no, love. In my book, you're living rough!

JACKIE: I like nice cosmetics, but I don't have time to go shopping. I do cleanse and moisturise these days. However, I don't really believe in the power of creams to keep you looking young. As long as it's got a bit of lard in it, then it's fine with me.

SHERRIE: I was on a programme last year called *Murder Most Famous* and it was the most wonderful thing I've ever done in my life, because we had to work with forensics and pathologists and people that you would never usually meet. Going behind the scenes and seeing the secret stuff was pretty mind-blowing.

Anyway, there were six of us and one of them was Diarmuid Gavin, the Irish gardener, who is just the sweetest heart, one of the loveliest men I've ever met in my life. One day we were with Minette Walters the writer, and Minette said to us, 'I want you to turn to the person next to you and say what you see and who you see. Diarmuid, you turn to Sherrie.'

Diarmuid turned to me and said something like, 'She has lovely eyes and if you look into those eyes, you can see right into her soul. You can see the unhappiness; you can see what she's been through; you can see everything in those eyes.'

Minette said something like, 'Yes, all right, and what's the bad bit?'

'She wears too much makeup,' he said, 'because that's her mask.' Everybody gasped.

Minette said, 'I agree.'

'What?' I said.

'It's a mask,' he went on, 'and you hide behind it. You don't need that amount of makeup, but you put it on, because the more you put on, the more you're getting rid of you.'

'You're very clever, Diarmuid,' Minette said, 'I can see that.'

I've been told this before, and I agree. But does it make me wear less makeup? No!

CAROL: What are you hiding, Sherrie? Is there some kind of maniac lurking under all the slap?

SHERRIE: Maybe there is, and maybe you'll find out one day! Grrr!

CAROL: Ooh, scary! Actually, I probably would be scared if I saw you without your makeup on. As for me, I don't like makeup very much.

SHERRIE: Whereas I've always felt I had to wear it, especially when I was playing Maureen opposite Reg Holdsworth in *Coronation Street*. We were quite big characters, so we were spread across papers and magazines every day of our lives.

I'd been an actress for twenty years before I went into the *Street* and I'd always done things that were quite high profile, but nothing like *Coronation Street*, which is like a business. Although I'd done drama and period series and sit-coms, I didn't understand what it meant to be in a soap. Because when you're in a soap, you open your bedroom window and there's a photographer sitting in a tree, looking at your bedroom window.

I kept forgetting. So one day I opened my bedroom window wearing hardly anything and the photographer was so shocked by this woman with no clothes on that he fell out of the tree! My husband then had to get him by the scruff of the neck and take him to hospital, because he had broken his leg. It was the funniest thing. We never stopped laughing about it.

So I learned that, whatever you do, before you open a window or pull back a curtain, put some makeup on! If you've got some makeup on, then at least they are taking a picture of somebody who has made an effort.

It became a joke with my husband and me. He'd say, 'You're not going to put your makeup on just to go and empty the bins, are you?'

But I knew that if I didn't, honest to god, I would open my door, walk down the drive and there would be somebody there with a camera. People will do anything to get a photograph.

It didn't actually bother me too much. I kind of thought it was hysterical that somebody could be so desperate to get a photograph of me that they'd sit in a tree or a bush. Also, that's the business we're in. You should be damn grateful that they're actually watching you, liking you and wanting an autograph!

THE THINGS PEOPLE SAY . . .

JANE: People don't think about what they're saying sometimes. I remember I was doing a club in Ossett in Wakefield once. I was in my early twenties, just a young slip of a thing. My uncle came to see me and he said, 'Oh dear, you've got your mother's knees.' It's silly really, because I've got quite shapely legs, but since that day, I've always worn tights or stockings. It affected me that much!

CAROL: And I was completely traumatised when one of the women on this panel revealed in the newspapers that I've got a bunion. Now everybody looks at my feet all the time. That was you, Jane!

JANE: Oh yes, but you've said it on the programme.

CAROL: It's true, I have, and it's also true that comments people make stay with you. I was at the seaside when I was younger, and I was wearing a very short red and white T-shirt dress and a very long plastic mac. A bloke pointed at the backs of my legs and said, 'Eurgh, you've got dimples on the backs of your legs!'

'Yeah, I know. They've been there all my life!'

Afterwards I went home and looked in the mirror. In fact, for about ten years after that, all I did was look at the backs of my legs in the mirror, thinking, Oh no, I've got dimples on the backs of my legs! For years I wore long skirts to hide them.

SHERRIE: Do you think about it now?

CAROL: Not really, no. I don't really care. I have still got dimples on the backs of my legs, like most women have in the wrong light. You can't let it get you down. What can you do about it?

ANDREA: You know that photo, where you flashed your bum and everyone saw your lovely pants? Maybe that bloke from the seaside was looking at that and thinking, Hey, I got it wrong all those years ago!

CAROL: No, he was thinking, I told her! I told her back in 1976 that there were dimples on the back of her legs!

SHERRIE: It hurts, doesn't it? I've had three things happen to me in my life that have never left me. The first was when I was very young and somebody said that I had hands like a navvy.
   The second was the time I met up with my ex-husband and he said, 'You've put weight on and you're not as good-looking as you used to be.'
   Thirdly, some old boyfriend told a newspaper, 'She used to be a bit of all right, but she's lost it.'

JANE: How rude!

 SHERRIE: Yes, how rude, and it sticks with you! Jibes really can destroy you. You think, How silly is that? But they don't go away, do they? They stay with you and you cannot get rid of them. I've tried, but it's impossible.

BAD HABITS

COLEEN: Jane cleanses, tones and moisturises every night, and then she moisturises her hands and feet. But sometimes I leave my makeup on all night. I love it, because when I have my makeup done professionally for *Loose Women*, it lasts two days!

DENISE: I'm terrible when it comes to blackheads. When Matthew was little, he used to say, 'Mummy, don't do your blackheads until I get home!' That's really quite disgusting, isn't it?

My mum was terrible. She was once on a bus, many years ago, and there was this guy in front of her who had blackheads all over his neck. Well, Mum had to sit on her hands to stop herself reaching out and squeezing them. So it's obviously something that runs in the family.

What else do I do? I'm terrible for picking the hard skin on my feet, and I like Tim to pick it as well. If Matthew sees my foot he yells, 'Nooo!' because he thinks I'm going to make him pick off the hard skin.

HAIR STORIES

COLEEN: When perms were fashionable in the 1970s, I went to the hairdresser's for a perm and came out looking like Kevin Keegan. It wasn't a good look. It was raining, and the hairdresser said, 'You can borrow an umbrella if you like.'

I thought, I don't want an umbrella! I wanted to wash it out. So I stood outside in the rain getting drenched. Unfortunately, being a perm, it just went frizzy.

JACKIE: Yes, I've had my fair share of tragic perms. The 1980s and the early 1990s weren't my strongest period, beauty-wise.

COLEEN: I like going to the hairdresser now, though. It helps that, as you get older, you stop trying to follow trends. You know what's going to suit you. So I'm not going to go and have a Victoria Beckham pixie cut, because I know it won't suit me. But if I were eighteen, I probably would try it.

I never had a Lady Di, though, because I never liked that hairstyle, although a lot of my friends did. I was more into perms and colours. I've been blonde; I've been all sorts of colours.

When I was eighteen, I had blonde highlights put in. I was still touring with my sisters at the time and I remember the papers all described me as 'Coleen, the vivacious blonde.' I think they thought I really was blonde. I definitely prefer being brunette. I think you get taken more seriously.

LYNDA: For me as well, the colour or cut of my hair used to make a big difference, or so it seemed. When I was twenty and left drama school, I was told by a casting director that I wouldn't work until I was forty, because I had a big face, an old face. He said that I wasn't pretty enough, and yet I wasn't ugly enough to be a character actress at that point. He wiped me out in one fell swoop, really.

Luckily, when you're younger, you don't believe in failure. You just don't see it. He's wrong! I thought.

I learnt very quickly that the best way to get through this not-being-pretty-enough was to do comedy, because you could glam me up for comedy. In the 1970s, comedy in this country was seaside-postcard-type comedy, tits and ass stuff. Inevitably they put a blonde wig on you, so I treated it like a character part: I was doing a character-acting role. I did a series for Jimmy Tarbuck very early on and played old women, young women, all kinds – but mostly blonde women. It was absolutely marvellous! This was what actors did, I thought.

I went on doing comedy for most of the 1970s and soon found to my horror that I'd got this image as a rather dumb blonde. I wasn't even blonde! That had to be remedied. So I went off and cut my hair off. Of course, the trouble then was that I was up a blind alley. If you did 'glamorous' comedy, nobody took you seriously as an actress.

I went blonde again for a Dry Cane rum commercial that was shot in Barbados. I was playing an English rose – me! – and of course they dyed my hair blonde, which led on to me being cast in *Confessions of a Driving Instructor*, the nadir of my career. There I was, stuck as a dumb blonde again. The Royal Shakespeare Company was never going to see me. I was completely f*****, really. So I went off and cut my hair short again. The next thing was, I got this series called *Funny Man* for Thames Television, playing Jimmy Jewel's daughter-in-law. It was brilliant!

COSMETIC SURGERY

SHERRIE: When my marriage ended, I went through a very bad time. I didn't know what would help. I wanted to be somebody else. So I decided to have some work done on my face. The idea was that I would wake up and look in the mirror and a new me would be staring back. It doesn't work like that. You have gone through all that and nothing has changed. It's the same old you, except you're now swollen like a distressed

turnip. I can laugh now but then it was hard to cope. If you have anything done it should be for the right reasons, not because of some man or to escape heartache. Yes it may make you feel a bit better about yourself and give you some confidence back. A little help or a little iron, as I call it, is fine. If you research it properly and you're confident in the person who will do the work, that's okay. As long as you know that it's only the outside and it's got nothing to do with what's going on inside.

JACKIE: Well, we think your insides are lovely, Sherrie.

JANE: As are your outsides! You're doing well, kid.

SHERRIE: There was an article in a magazine recently that said I've had liposuction, which I've never had, and lip enhancement, which I've never had, but about five years ago I had a chemical peel, which was fantastic.

COLEEN: I'm not against cosmetic surgery. Each to their own. And I'm all for it if you've had a disfigurement or even just a nose that has blighted your life.

What I am against is young girls in their early twenties having liposuction because it's easier than dieting and eating properly, or because Katie Price has done it. One minute they are having their boobs enlarged and the next minute they are having the implants taken out. All of this worries me, because if they're struggling with body issues in their early to mid-twenties, Christ knows what they going to be doing when they are forty-three, like me. By then, they would have had it all done, so what's next? It's almost become like going shopping.

In my mum's day, nobody had cosmetic surgery and you just accepted people for what they were. You'd say, 'She doesn't look great for her age,' or, 'God, she looks good for eighty-five!'

Now you say, 'She looks good. What is she, about forty?' And someone replies, 'No she's eighty-five.'

I can understand why people are doing it, but I'm frightened that we're all going to end up looking like *The Stepford Wives*, and no one is going to be able to tell anyone's age.

A lot of the time you can tell if someone's had surgery. People get obsessed with it. First they tell you, 'I'm just having my eyes done.' Then six months down the line they say, 'Well, that was so good I'm going to have my  nose done now.' They end up looking totally over the top, like Joan Rivers. I just wish we could accept that we can't be perfect.

JACKIE: I'm with you there, Coleen. I'm not against cosmetic surgery, but I think some people go too far. It can become an addiction. When people start getting addicted to cosmetic surgery, they kind of lose perspective of what's an improvement. Then they start to look nonhuman. I've seen my fair share of it in America, but I think this country's becoming accustomed to cosmetic surgery too. You quite often see celebs who have gone one procedure too far.

COLEEN: I have to admit that the other reason I'm not having it done is because I'm a coward. I don't even like going to the dentist, so to voluntarily go and put myself through a general anaesthetic and stitches is not my idea of a good day out.

DENISE: I had my eyes done last year. It's interesting, because even though the change is quite subtle, it really has made a difference. Nobody would say, 'God, you've had your eyes done!' but I definitely think I look a little bit healthier. My surgeon said, 'I can't give you the *wow* effect because your bags are not that bad. What I can do is make people say, "You look really well!"'

We have a tendency for quite dark shadowing in our family

and I looked tired a lot of the time, even when I wasn't. So it has just kind of freshened things up a bit. If I've had a big night out, I look slightly less hanging than I did six months ago, before I had it.

It was worth it but for a while I didn't know if I'd done the right thing, because you look pretty grotesque when you've had it done, even though the surgeon's work was incredible. I've had hardly any scarring and hardly any bruising, and I was back at work within two weeks.

To be honest, when I look at the episode of *Loose Women* when I'd just had it done, I just look wrong. What have I done? I thought. I look horrendous. But then gradually it settles over about six months.

I know quite a lot about cosmetic surgery, because I did the voiceover for the Channel 4 programme, *10 Years Younger*. Apparently it's normal to think, What have I done to my face? immediately after the operation.

I went to see someone as research for another programme I was presenting. She said, 'As you get older, you need the edges of your mouth lifted a little bit.'

Since I'm the sort of person who likes to wear new shoes out of the shop, I said, 'Go on, then.'

But when I walked into the house, my son said, 'Mum, can we discuss why you've turned into the Joker from Batman?' I immediately burst into tears.

The next day it was fine, but whenever I looked in the mirror, I saw the Joker and thought, Oh my god what have I done?

JANE: Like Denise, immediately after I had my eyes done, I looked at myself and thought, Did I fall off the trolley? But every day, as you can see it getting better, you think, Wow!!

As long as you feel better, that's all that matters. It's all about how you feel, not whether everybody else says, 'Oh my god, that's fantastic!' If you look in the mirror and you're happy with what you see, then it has worked.

I say yes to cosmetic surgery, if it works for you. There are a lot of people it doesn't work for, but not everybody is blessed with great genes. I wasn't, as you saw on *The Cruise*.

I'm very happy, and confidence is a wonderful thing, but I did go through a patch where I just looked really tired and old. I had big bags under my eyes, so I had a little bit done to them, the same as Denise.

I'm very happy with it, because I don't look so tired all the time now. There's a difference with corrective and plastic, I think. I just had a slight alteration, that's all.

DENISE: I'm very glad I had it done too. It has got to be something to do with this reversal in fortunes I'm experiencing, as regards attention from men, unless I'm just giving off more of a confident vibe. Maybe I am because I feel more confident.

I'd thought about having it done for years and just never did. I'd had like fillers and a bit of Botox here and there, but I hadn't actually had any surgery. Maybe it was something to do with being fifty.

JACKIE: If I ever had cosmetic surgery, I wouldn't admit it! I don't see the point. I'd rather people just thought I looked refreshed. I also think anything you do with your own body is your own business. I think it's fine if people do admit it, though. Denise has spoken about it on the show and she looks great. She looks well rested and refreshed.

LYNDA: I hate it when people don't admit it! Or if they claim their shape is all down to genes and luck and they don't have to work at it at all. Jane Fonda went on about her healthy lifestyle while she was secretly suffering from bulimia. Women are under so much pressure.

I'm quite happy with what I look like at sixty. Candice Bergen, who is in *Boston Legal*, is an example of an older woman who looks amazing without cosmetic surgery.

Whether I'll be happy with what I look like at seventy is another matter, but I don't see the point in messing around with your body surgically, because it can go so wrong. You can disguise a multitude of sins with clothes, so I certainly wouldn't do it.

COLEEN: People probably say that I look much slimmer in the flesh than I do on the telly because the desk comes to just under my boobs, so all they see are these ginormous boobs and they assume that the rest of me follows suit.

I'm now a size ten overall, but my shirt size is still a twelve or fourteen because of my boobs. In the process of losing weight, I've lost a bit of weight off them too, and now I'm realising that they're heading south slightly. So the other day I was thinking I might have to have a bit of a lift, but then I thought, No, I can't, I'm too scared!

LYNDA: Me too, although I can understand it, especially if you've been incredibly beautiful. But it appals me because it can go so wrong. At the end of the day, I don't care what anybody says, they can't guarantee that they will achieve what they show you on a piece of paper.

Once you've had plastic surgery, you've got to keep having it done, and when your face is Botoxed to hell, you have your neck done, and then you start working your way down. Apparently they can do something with your hands as well. I've heard of at least one actress having her hands burnt to make them look younger. Of course, I do it all the time – on the iron and the oven!

You have to wonder what's going on in the heads of people who have masses of plastic surgery. If they're doing it because the man in their life has a) told them to, or b) made them feel they should have it done, invariably he leaves them for the younger model in the end anyway. So they're on a hiding to nothing.

He can go off with a thirty-five-year-old when he's sixty, but you're not ever going to get a thirty-five-year-old, unless he's after your money. Joan Collins is an exception, I suppose. She's beautiful. Still, you're going to get old no matter what. You cannot ultimately hold it at bay.

I went to see a man about Botox once. He peered at me and said, 'Yes, you're absolutely right! You're ready for a facelift.'

'I don't want a facelift!' I said. 'I'm talking about Botox in my forehead.'

He froze the little frown line between my eyebrows and it did get rid of the frown. But that's all I wanted. I didn't want my eyes to go up at the sides as well, which is always a telltale sign, isn't it? I had this clamped eyes-open look, rabbit-in-the-headlights; I looked permanently surprised after the treatment. It's true that it works, but you can't do anything with your face so, in a way, it didn't do what it was supposed to do. It hurt, too. They say it doesn't hurt, but it did. It made my eyes water. I never went back for more. I now proudly carry my frown line.

DENISE: If you have it done by the best people, they do it to the point that you don't lose the expression in your face. Mine has been done just subtly enough that I don't lose any expression. I have two people that do my Botox, one in the north and one in the south, but I'm not somebody that goes every three months. Some people go off and have it done as soon as a single line appears again, but I'm not that bothered about it.

People say, 'You look really well, Den,' rather than, 'Have you had something done?'

It's just amazing how the lines just vanish before your eyes. Suddenly, they're gone! So why not, I say?

LYNDA: The jaw line is the most obvious thing to have done. You think, If I could only just have that little bit lifted! It's a very clever procedure. It gives you definition. But I think that once you start, you can't stop.

It's all very well for me, people might say, because I've just got married again and somebody loves me for the way I am. Having said that, he loves to look at beautiful women, but what's nice is that he can look at them and share it with me without making me feel inadequate or insecure about it.

What we've got is a relationship that I know he wouldn't have with anybody else, and it's not based on what we look like. He's no oil painting, after all! That's the thing, isn't it? How dare men make their other half feel insecure as they get steadily paunchier?

Women make each other feel insecure, but there are a

lot of men who have a problem with getting old themselves and want the younger model. They project that onto the other half, even unwittingly. You want to say to them, 'Go away, mate, and sort yourself out before you tell me what to do!'

We remarked on someone being very beautiful the other day and I said, 'You can hold that thought when we go to bed tonight.'

'I don't need to fantasise!' he said. 'I'd rather have my wife.'

GETTING OLDER

LYNDA: We all know that getting old is horrible and there's no need to go on about it the whole time. You have to accentuate the positives, even though they're quite hard to find sometimes!

Having said that, women over fifty are completely ignored by society. You've done all the hard work, you've brought up the children, you've run the home and then suddenly you're completely invisible.

DENISE: From the age of forty-five to fifty, I felt invisible. No matter how happily married you are, as a woman you still want to feel attractive. It's quite nice to have a flirt, a harmless flirt, every now and then. It can be difficult if you've never had a problem getting boys and suddenly the attention isn't there. I thought, god it's happened! Knowing that this is when it happens doesn't help you when it happens.

But then, suddenly, at fifty, I find it's gone the other way.

I've recently had a couple of texts from people saying that they fancy me. I'm not going to do anything about it, but it's very nice! One thing I do enjoy about ageing is that I'm more confident in my own skin.

LYNDA: I'm quite lucky because I'm on the telly. I'm only visible because people recognise me. It's interesting how that then develops: a young student, say, will start off tolerating me because they've seen me on the telly, but then you can see them thinking, Oh, she's not too bad; she's quite funny really. She's gone out, got drunk and had sex like the rest of us.

DENISE: I think the word fifty is worse than the reality of being fifty. If I see it written down – 'Fifty-year-old Doris Metcalf . . .' – I feel as if I'm reading about someone my mother's age, not mine.

In fact, this is actually one of the best years I've had. I feel I've regressed in age. Perhaps that, and my absolute party mania this year, are connected to the freedom that I've had from my illness. I used to have to be careful with hangovers. I knew that if I had a bad hangover or I'd been on an all-nighter and therefore was sleep-deprived that I was more than likely to induce depression. Being free of that means that now I can think of myself as a normal person that can go out and get wrecked!

WHAT DO YOU THINK OF AIRBRUSHING ON MAGAZINE COVERS?

SHERRIE: It was funny the other day, because I saw this woman on a magazine cover. She's forty-five or forty-six and she looked ten. I thought, How sad, because you can't see who she is.

Don't get me wrong, I always tell them to airbrush me, but that's me! They can airbrush me as much as they like, but when I see other people I think, Oh dear, I can't see who you are, because it's a doll-like version of you. I think it's bizarre. There's no personality there, nothing. It's just like having a model and I think it's wrong. So I like to be airbrushed, but I don't think anybody else should be.

DENISE: Bring it on! I don't mind it at all. I know they say that young girls are aspiring to be the kind of flawless people they see on the covers of magazines, but I think that most people do know that the image has been enhanced. You can always tell if a photo is airbrushed.

I don't think I would have wanted it so much when I was young, but I don't mind a little bit of it now, and I wouldn't mind if they elongated my legs into the bargain!

Chapter 3

Feeling Good

Hup, two-three-four! And stretch, two-three-four! Are you crunching those abs? Firming those thighs? No? Hey, we don't blame you! Sometimes life seems too short to suffer a gruelling regime of sweaty workouts and hunger pangs. Although we know from our own chequered history with fitness that if you find a way of exercising that works for you and stick at it, it can leave you feeling amazing. We'd never be ones to get obsessed with keeping fit, though, and always remind each other that pampering yourself is good for you too. So every now and then, why not flop down and have a massage instead? Go on, you deserve it. A little bit of what you fancy does you good – and it will leave you glowing.

Follow our tips for showing off your best bits and stop obsessing about the bits you're less keen on. Nobody else is paying half as much attention to them as you are, trust us. Learn how to dress to flaunt what you've got and share in our joy of shopping. Beware the deadly changing rooms, though. It only takes one bad mirror to send you running to the lettuce aisle, sobbing . . .

We're strong believers in the fact that it's what's inside that counts, but there's no harm in making sure the packaging is as appealing as possible!

EXERCISE

COLEEN: Posture makes all the difference to how you look. My trainer is constantly telling me, 'Sit up properly and pull your shoulders back! You see? You already look like you've lost a stone!'

LYNDA: I have got this amazing girl who trains with me. It's very grand to say she's my personal trainer. She is a personal trainer, but she's had children over the last eight years we've been together, so it's good for her as well if we exercise together.

COLEEN: My trainer is lovely and very fit, but he's gay, so I can flirt as much as I want but I ain't going to make myself attractive to him. I'm married, so I wouldn't be interested anyway, but I like the fact that I know I'm not going to get anywhere, because it's almost like training with my best friend, without any embarrassment. Unfortunately, I only get to see him when he's teaching me a new routine for one of my fitness DVDs, so I make sure I really get the most out of him!

I think if he were good-looking and straight, it would be a little embarrassing. Some of the positions you get into when you're training are not very elegant! Last week, while he was stretching me out and lying on top of me, pushing my legs back, I said, 'God, it's just as well you're gay, or my husband might divorce me if he walked in now!'

CAROL: I don't have a personal trainer – I look after myself. I often go to the gym and have a sauna. I walk there and back and it's a good mile and a half away, so I don't need to work out when I get there. My routine is always exactly the same. The sauna and shower always makes me feel better and saves a hell of a lot on hot-water bills at home.

SHERRIE: I'd love to do *Strictly Come Dancing*, because my parents were ballroom dancers and I used to do the cha-cha-cha with my dad.

I was watching it last year and I don't know how old Cherie Lunghi is, but she looked fantastic on it. That started me thinking about exercise and I thought about how if I were offered *Strictly* . . . it would make me go to a gym three times a week and tone up every part of my body, even my bat wings.

I would stick to a regime because I'd know I was going to be on the show. It would be a great motivator.

So then I had a really big row with myself that went like this:

'Why don't you do it anyway?'

'Well, I would do, of course, but I work so hard . . . (touch wood).'

'But why don't you start going, even if it's once a week? You could say, "Right, you boy, good-looking boy, come over here and tone me up!"'

So maybe I will, now I've had a good talk to myself. But I might need an incentive like a show. I'd love a magazine to ring me and say, 'We're going to tone you up to show somebody of your age how you can be totally toned.'

Otherwise, I won't do it, because by the time I get home, I'm so tired that I don't move. Still, I'd love somebody to tone me up. It would be wonderful to have a body that didn't look its age.

JACKIE: When I was in America I was pretty fit. What worked for me was hiking up the canyons in LA. I like the outdoors and the fresh air. When I get the chance in Scotland at weekends and we've got a bit of help with the kids I like to go hill walking.

I'm not very good at gyms. I find gyms tedious. They've always got mirrored walls, haven't they? Well, it's not motivational for me to see myself looking fat and sweaty and red-faced in the mirror as I'm pounding away.

Since I've had my kids, my exercise is trailing up and down the stairs with various babies in arms. Strangely enough, I'm probably the thinnest I've ever been, but it's all flab.

I don't feel fit. It would be nice to be able to get back to peak fitness at some point, if only because it would make me feel more energetic. I'd like to have a bit more vim and vigour, instead of slogging my way through the day. I have a great time with the kids, but it does take every ounce of energy.

Most relatively new mothers will relate to it when I say that you're tired all the time. It would be nice to have time to get fit, but if you have a spare moment, you just want to sleep or catch up on household chores.

DENISE: My bouts of exercising are very intermittent. I'm always on a roll and then I go and have a party night and smoke too much, which sets me back. Then I can't be bothered to do it for another couple of weeks. My trainer, Sal, says I'm the worst client she's ever had because I never go training with her. I just say in a whisper, 'Let's have a glass of wine instead . . .'

All the same, I love it when I'm in exercise mode. I love the fact I did the Great Wall of China last year. Well, I didn't do the whole wall, obviously: it's four thousand miles long. But I was so proud of myself that I managed to average twelve kilometres a day on the unreconstructed parts, which are much harder than the stretches of tourist wall, which they call the Disney bit of the wall.

I wasn't fit enough when I did it and I can't explain how hard it was. I admit that I threw my toys out of the pram a couple of times because it was so difficult. A lot of the time I didn't care about being on one of the Seven Wonders of the World. My cousin's wife, Fran, who came with us, said

that she heard me mumbling, 'Who built this f***** b*****
wall?' as I brought up the rear!

We didn't camp but we stayed in very basic accommodation.
There was one place that was just like Norman Bates's hotel
in *Psycho*. It was scary. So some of us got drunk that night.
You almost had to get drunk in order to be able to sleep in
that bed. We drank this stuff they had behind the bar; it had
probably been there for a hundred years because nobody was
stupid enough to drink it. We discovered later that it had
donkey penis, tiger's bollocks, intestines and some bit of dog
in it. Only men were supposed to drink it, and they were
only meant to drink a small shot for their sexual prowess!

It makes me feel a bit sick thinking about how we downed
shot after shot, little knowing what it contained or what it
was for. We got so pissed that it all went off and we formed
the LRA that night, the Lesbian Ramblers' Association. We
were going to get T-shirts printed with LRA on it and
everything – funny how carried away you can get with totally
bonkers schemes after you've had a few . . .

Next came drink and dial, drink and dial. I phoned my
driver Gary and when I got back to England, he said, 'You
should make sure you put your phone down at the end of a
conversation.' Apparently, he had heard me shouting, 'What
the hell are we all doing in bloody China when we could be
shagging on a beach in the sunshine?'

The next morning was terrible. I mean, I've felt like that
and had to go to work and managed it and I've had to look
after my children and managed it. But that morning we made
the one-thousand-step ascent to the Great Wall and then
had to walk for twelve kilometres in the worst wind and rain
that you can imagine. At one point, I just thought it would

be preferable to jump off the wall, because I couldn't face any more blooming steps and at least it would be a memorable way to go! I'd much rather that than being run over by a bus in Rochdale, to be honest.

But by the end of that day, I thought, I can get through anything now. When I get back from China I'm going to join the real Ramblers' Association (sobriety the morning after the night before led to a very quick disbandment of the LRA . . .), and I'm going to be out there every Saturday, walking my socks off.

Fast forward to Saturday a week later, back home after an all-nighter in Manchester: 'Darling, will you just get me some Alka-Seltzer? Please! I can't move off the sofa.' I never did join the Ramblers' Association . . .

ALTERNATIVE THERAPY/MASSAGE

DENISE: If I had to choose between not having sex again and not having a massage again, I'd be really torn. Massage is my most favourite thing in the entire world. I could be massaged 24/7, all year round, and never get tired of it. Not sure I feel quite the same about sex!

COLEEN: I love having a massage. It is such a luxury. I don't go a lot, though. In fact, I can't remember the last time I had a massage. When I think about it, I decide that, yes, I'm going to treat myself! But I still find it hard to live in the 'celeb world of treatments'.

My thinking is that there is so much other stuff I could

buy for the price of one massage. It's just something that was drummed into me when I was young. I grew up with my mother saying, 'Girl, you've more money than sense!' That has stayed with me, which means I always decide that there are better things I can spend my money on.

It's funny, because I hesitate about paying someone sixty or seventy pounds to massage me for an hour, but I would spend the same amount on my children or my husband at the drop of a hat. So I'm not holding back because the money will go towards a bill. I'm just in that maternal phase in my life where you treat everyone else and don't really treat yourself.

My advice to someone in my position would be to try and take an hour a day, or an hour every couple of days, to think about yourself or do something for yourself. But I know how hard it is. You just don't. For me, it's not about being a martyr. It's just that I get more enjoyment out of looking after them than doing things just for myself.

SHERRIE: The idea of having a massage is wonderful, but somebody else would have to book it and take me there. I couldn't do it myself. I would never go. I'd book it and then lose the money, because I wouldn't turn up.

The idea is wonderful, but for me the reality doesn't match. I've had a couple of massages and I don't really enjoy it. I generally find they're too weak and don't do it hard enough, although I wouldn't like somebody who was so powerful that it hurt.

DENISE: My trainer is also a sports masseuse. She says that of all the people she has massaged, including rugby players, she has never known anyone to take pressure on their shoulders like me. Honestly, three grown men could stand on my shoulders and I'd be asking them to press just a little bit harder.

I like a firm massage, but I don't like it when it hurts. I thought I was going to punch one particular masseuse in China. She massaged me after the walk and it was so hard I wanted to fight her, I really did.

JACKIE: I love Thai massage; it's a bit of an indulgence for me. Some people call it 'fat man's yoga' or 'lazy man's yoga'.

You do it fully clothed, wearing pyjamas or a tracksuit. You get stretched into yoga positions and have all of your muscles massaged so that they can loosen up. I absolutely love it. When I come down to London to do *Loose Women*, I'll sometimes have a two-hour Thai massage. I have been known to have a three-hour massage on a bad day, which the girls can't believe!

JANE: Three hours is a heck of a long time to be having your muscles massaged, love. Do they have to work in shifts?

SHERRIE: I just wouldn't have the patience for that. I'm sure my mind would keep wandering, and then I'd want to wander off. I've never had reflexology in my life, or aromatherapy, or anything like it. People always say that I'm the kind of person it was made for, because of my hypertension. I'm always hyper, always buzzing, and when I come down I just become comatose. So reflexology was made for me. I would love to try it, it's just a matter of making the time.

DENISE: I'm very open to trying anything for anything, because I do think a lot of it is psychological. If you think it's going to work, a lot of the time it's going to work.

I tried acupuncture for my lower back once. It didn't really work; there doesn't seem to be much anyone can do for backs, apart from manipulation.

I love reflexology, but I think that's because somebody's playing with my feet, and I love having my feet played with!

LYNDA: I love massage. My treat on tour is to seek out the spa and have massages and facials there. A lot of pampering is a good thing.

I'll try anything; I'll give anything a whirl. Acupuncture worked when I had a bad back and I'd rather do that than take pills, obviously.

The great thing about massage and other non-surgical treatments is they might work, they don't do any harm, they feel brilliant and so why not?

PAMPERING

COLEEN: How do I pamper myself? Every Monday night I stay in London at a lovely hotel, after coming down to film *Loose Women*. That's pamper enough for me. I can lie on that bed after my shower and watch what I want and not move. Just that one night a week is like a little holiday, because I haven't got the kids and I'm not thinking that I'd better put the washing on or unload the dishwasher. Instead I've got room service! So I sit there like a slob. It's fantastic.

GUIDE TO SHOWING YOUR BEST BITS AND HIDING YOUR WORST BITS

COLEEN: First you need to discover what your best bits and worst bits are, and be really honest with yourself. For instance, I've never gone out in hipsters and a top showing off my midriff, because I know that would just make people sick, including myself.

I saw so many people walking round town when that look was in fashion, and it didn't suit even some of the young girls, because they had rolls of fat bulging out. You just think, *No!* I know it's in fashion, but only if you're a size eight!

But once you get to know your own body, you can still look fashionable, without looking ridiculous.

JACKIE: If I feel rough or I'm not looking my best and I have to go out into the world, I tend to wear something sparkly to throw people off the scent. When I'm working, I am fully made up and looking glamorous thanks to scores of professionals! So when I'm at home, for me to register that it's a day off, I go to the other extreme and tend to wear no makeup, ponytail, jeans and a jumper. My poor husband.

SHERRIE: As you get older, the tummy that you once had as a little girl comes back and becomes distended. I assume it's partly because of diet and perhaps things like wheat allergies, and also because your muscles loosen when you get older and are no longer taut.

So I tend to wear things that don't show the midriff, because that's always a giveaway. I would never wear a bikini or a swimsuit. I would never wear anything on holiday like shorts or a miniskirt. I drive my mother mad, because I'm always covered up.

I wouldn't wear a backless dress these days, although I might go semi-backless, and I think there's nothing worse that seeing a person like me in a bikini. Mind you, look at Helen Mirren in that bikini photo – that was fantastic! She obviously keeps herself very toned.

SECRET TIPS TO LOOKING GOOD – SPANX PANTS

COLEEN: Good underwear is essential. If you're going to wear a tight slinky dress, make sure you've got the old Spanx pants on. I've only just discovered them recently and they're brilliant.

Any help you can get underneath the outfit is always handy, but make sure you get time to whip it off before your husband or boyfriend sees it, because it looks vile!

SHERRIE: I like Spanx pants, but it's as if they add a layer of skin, so you're adding more than you're actually taking away. Or at least that's how I think of them. I know Coleen thinks they're great and Denise wears them all the time, but for me they are the most uncomfortable pants I've ever worn. Horribly uncomfortable.

YOUR BEST AND WORST BITS – BUNIONS, ETC

SHERRIE: My best bits are my eyes and my back. That's it, really.

COLEEN: My best bits? Don't ask me. I don't know. In one way, my boobs are my best bit. They've always been a talking point, and sometimes it's great. But in another way they're my worst bit because they've been the bane of my life. Having bigger boobs can be very limiting and I think my posture is bad because of the size of them. It's all very well for my trainer to say, 'Put your shoulders back!' but when I do, it pushes out my boobs and I worry that I'm going to look like I'm saying, 'Hey, look at these babies!' That's why I tend to hunch up.

DENISE: Ah, but if you draw attention to your boobs, it will of course take attention away from other bits. Over the years my boobs have grown. I used to have no tits and now I've just got these *tits*, which is great! They're not great tits, but I can make them look good with the right sort of bra. I quite enjoy getting my tits out for the lads a bit, although not in a ridiculously over-the-top way.

The one bit I hate about the ageing thing is arms. When I was in *Coronation Street*, I was known for wearing sleeveless dresses. Jaci Stephen used to call me 'the phantom sleeve cutter', because I cut the sleeves out of all my tops.

I became known for it in the press and people thought that I worked out because of my arms. They always seemed to look naturally toned, even though I never did any exercise when I was in *Coronation Street*. But now gravity has done its work . . .

However, the trainer I worked with for the *Woman* magazine diet told me that in just a few sessions I would get that definition back. So maybe I'll give it a try. I don't want to have to wear long sleeves all the time.

JANE: I've no choice, love. My worst bits are my bingo wings, so I tend to wear long sleeves if I can. There's nothing you can do about them, unfortunately. I don't care what anybody says: you can pick up as many tins of beans as you want, but it's not going to get rid of them.

I've got a little bum, which is quite lucky, so that might be my best bit. I've got long legs too. I'm not in Carol McGiffin's league for legs, but I'm very happy with them. I've got quite an average body, so I'm all right. I'm very happy with being a normal size twelve.

DENISE: I used to hate having a round face. I always put weight on my face. Now I'm really glad I've got a round face when I look at people who have incredibly thin faces because they're ageing really badly. Other parts of them aren't ageing badly, but it is really showing on their face. So I'm quite glad now that I've got that little bit of plumpness there.

ANDREA: At certain times of the months I get spots and when I'm tired I get spots. Everyone has their thing and that's mine. I had terrible spots when I was at school and it upset me, like it upset everybody, but I was quite a cheerful upbeat person and I don't remember it ever really getting me down. I was a very busy teenager. I liked sport, drama, art and public speaking and I had something on every night after school. I didn't really have time to think about myself.

When I look back at pictures of myself, I'm astounded at how confident I was. Years later my mum said to me that there were days when my face looked so bad that she considered keeping me off school, because I used to get bullied. It got me down, but it never occurred to me why they were bullying me. When they called me 'Spotty', I thought it was because I was different to them, because I grew up abroad, had a funny accent and had a strange outlook on life.

My parents used to say that it was just because they were jealous. I would look in the mirror and think, What are they jealous of? If they'd actually spoken to me, they'd have seen that there was nothing to be jealous of at all. I was just a busy person.

Although I have always been a glass half-full person, it was absolutely hideous being picked on at school. It was scary as well. I had never seen so much hatred before. It was horrible – you know how girls can get. It made me withdraw into myself and put me off being the centre of attention.

That's why I tend to be cautious. I dip my toe in and make sure that it's okay, not show off exactly, but to shine. I would never walk into a crowded room and go, 'Hi!' in case people hated me for it. I'd rather make sure that everyone's okay with me first.

SHOULD YOU DRESS FOR YOUR AGE? HOW?

SHERRIE: I wouldn't wear a miniskirt or hot pants, like I used to; I wouldn't wear fluffy frilly and I wouldn't wear smocky. It's quite rare for me to wear a dress. When I do, it's likely to be Italian and very well cut. I'm careful about not looking like mutton dressed as lamb.

I've got a lot of All Saints jewellery. I love it and I get letters all the time from *Loose Women* viewers, saying, 'Could you tell us where you get your necklaces from?'

I was wearing an All Saints necklace recently and a friend asked where it was from. When I told her, she said, 'Oooh, a bit trendy for your age!'

'Shut up, what do you mean my age?' I said.

'I didn't mean it like that,' she said. 'I meant that All Saints is a bit kiddy young!'

Personally, I don't consider All Saints that young. I just think it's unusual, but I know what she means.

RETAIL THERAPY

JANE: I love shopping, but if I find something I like, I tend to think, Right, I'll have three of those, or I'll have that in three colours; especially when I find a pair of jeans that look great, because you don't often get a really good pair of jeans. I'm bad like that.

I never regret buying things. I'm always glad that I bought something because it means that I don't get up the next day wishing I'd got it. That's a worse feeling!

COLEEN: I hate clothes shopping. I can't bear it. I never liked it, even as a kid. I just find it boring. I'll only go shopping when there's an event coming up and I need an outfit. I don't understand browsing for hours on end in a shop. I just can't think of anything worse.

Having said that, I can shop all day for my little girl and I can shop all day for my boys and my husband. It's funny, but I actually love going shopping with them for their clothes, but it's the opposite when it comes to shopping for me. I've got my favourite clothes that I wear all the time – five or six tops and a couple of pairs of jeans – and that's enough.

JACKIE: Comfort eating, maybe; comfort shopping, no!

XMAS SHOPPING

COLEEN: Every year I decide that I'm going to have everything bought and wrapped by October, by the end of October at the latest. But every year I find myself going to the shops on Christmas Eve and wrapping my presents at the last minute.

I get very, very hassled and I moan and groan like everyone else, but I absolutely love Christmas. I love everything about it: the tree, Christmas dinner, even the shopping!

JACKIE: I do my Christmas shopping online, get it delivered and wrap it at home!

COLEEN: I'm usually pretty happy with the gifts Ray gives me on Christmas morning, but he spends the whole lead-up to Christmas from the beginning of December . . . he's a bit like you, Carol, a bit Bah! Humbug! about Christmas. He spends the whole time saying, 'I can't bear it. I'm so stressed. Don't talk about it. I can't handle it.' But the only presents he actually buys are for me! I buy all the family's presents, the kids' presents, all his family's presents, the dinner. He's only got one present to buy, for me, and he gets so stressed.

CAROL: It's difficult for blokes! Shopping doesn't come naturally to them, does it?

COLEEN: No, because they're idiots!

JACKIE: Do you give him a list, or do you tell him exactly what to go and get?

COLEEN: Well, I like surprises, so I'd hate to say to him, 'I want that,' because I'd go to bed on Christmas Eve knowing I've got that. So I give him a list of four or five things and I say, 'I don't want all of them, but just choose one, so I don't know what you're getting me.' Carol, stop looking at me like you're going to vomit!

CAROL: Did he ever get you anything that wasn't on the list that you thought was completely brilliant? Did he ever ad lib?

COLEEN: Oh yes, he'll get me one main present and then there'll be loads of other surprises and extra gifts that I don't know anything about.

JACKIE: Ah, that's nice! What about you, Jane? What's been your experience of being the recipient of a man's gift, in a manner of speaking?

JANE: Men just don't seem to get it right, do they? Especially when it comes to underwear. They don't seem to know your size, and it's always two sizes too small.

CAROL: They get the size they want you to be!

JANE: Is that what it was?

CAROL: Maybe Jane, I don't know, but they always get the scratchiest stuff, all scratchy up your backside.

JANE: Hmm, not good, is it?

COLEEN: You two are so going out with the wrong men!

JACKIE: Are you any good at buying gifts for men? Are you good at knowing what they want?

CAROL: I'm really good at presents. If I do have to buy something for someone, I put a lot of thought into it. If I was going out with someone who walked into the garage and picked something up on Christmas Eve and wrapped it and said, 'Er, here you go,' that would be it for me. I can't stand that lack of effort. He'd be out the door.

JACKIE: I think you're either the type of person who actually enjoys thinking about somebody's gift and going out to find it and wrapping it, or it's just a chore to you.

COLEEN: I think if most men were honest they would say it was just a chore for them.

CAROL: They don't like shopping, do they?

COLEEN: There's not many I've met who say, 'I love it!'

JANE: And it's so busy, and there's the parking and everything else . . .

CAROL: (sigh)

COLEEN: Oh my god, we're a bunch of right old miseries, aren't we?

JANE: . . . but a couple of years ago a boyfriend got me something that I really wanted.

COLEEN: Did he?

JANE: Steady . . . and I still play with it all the time! Wa-hey!

INTERNET SHOPPING

JANE: That's something I don't do. I like to touch, feel, see.
I'm not very good at buying anything off a page.

JACKIE: I do household and grocery shopping online and have
my groceries delivered, but I do most of my shopping for
clothes in railway stations and airports. Sometimes I'll only
have time for a quick browse, but if I don't buy it this week,
I know I'll be back next week. I wouldn't have had any clothes
for the past two years if I didn't get to go to airports.

I'm one of the few people who likes Terminal Five. I know
Carol thinks it was designed and built by the Antichrist, but
I'm actually thrilled to bits with it. Last summer I went away
for a few days and kitted myself out completely within an
hour and a half at Terminal Five: bikinis, dresses, sunglasses,
everything!

When I lived in LA, I was one of these people who would
go shopping in quite a big way twice a year. I don't really
like to browse. I'm not a go-to-the-shops-every-week type
of person. So I'd go once for the winter and once for the
summer, spend the whole day and do quite a lot of damage
on the credit card.

I'm the kind of person who will take thirty-five things into
the changing rooms and won't come out for an hour until
I've found something I like, much to the chagrin of the
assistants.

GIFTS – MOST EXTRAVAGANT GIFT BOUGHT/RECEIVED AND WORST GIFT RECEIVED

COLEEN: My husband Ray is a guitarist and I've bought him most of the guitars that he's wanted. Don't ask what they are because I don't know, but they're expensive. He in turn has given me some lovely jewellery and other extravagant treats.

In the run-up to Christmas one year, I kept saying, 'Right, as soon as Christmas is over, I'm going to get fit!'

So Ray decided to buy me a lot of keep-fit stuff as a Christmas present, like yoga videos and a keep-fit mat. But it's one thing you saying it, and another when your husband agrees with you . . . It made me think, Oh, so I am a big fat biffa, is what you're trying to tell me?

JANE: My worst gift was a book. I actually got nothing but *a book* for my Christmas present off someone. I just thought, Is that it? I looked at him. Yeah? Ten quid! It was a great book, but the person who gave it to me didn't even buy it himself. I hate it when no thought goes into a present.

JACKIE: The best present I've ever received are my children. I know that sounds ever so corny, but they were both born very close to my birthday in March, on two consecutive years. The best present I've ever given was on my husband's thirty-second birthday, when I gave him a son. I had actually bought him a golf bag, but a son kind of topped that! It took a lot of effort! I had a very long labour and he should really have been born the day before, but it was worth the wait. When my husband is fifty, my son will be eighteen, so I'm really looking forward to that party!

The most extravagant present I've ever given anyone was when I gave my mum and dad a six-week round-the-world trip a few years ago for their anniversary. I hope they made the most of it, because it's been socks and pants since then!

CHRISTMAS PRESENTS

COLEEN: I'm such a fan of Christmas. When we were younger it was very important, especially to my mum and dad. They were the glue at Christmas and we all used to gather at their house. I remember, as a kid, my mum cooked for between eighteen and twenty-four people in our little terraced house. She loved it. Well, she said she did! We went back for years and years. Then, when my dad passed away and my mum got ill, I really appreciated how they kept us together for Christmas, because then we all went off and did our own things with our own little families. We still try to get together on Christmas morning. After Santa's presents, we then go round one of our houses and open all the family presents.

CAROL: You pick everything up and carry it to someone else's house?

COLEEN: No, you idiot! Santa leaves the presents at all the kids' houses, obviously, and when we know which house we're going to, on Christmas Eve we deliver all our presents round to that one house.

CAROL: What a hassle! I thought Santa was supposed to do that.

COLEEN: He does deliver the kids' presents. Are you listening, cloth-ears?

JANE: I'm wondering how you seat twenty-four people in a terraced house?

COLEEN: Well, we had a very big table!

GUILTY PLEASURES

SHERRIE: My daughter and I are shopaholics. We love window shopping. I'm also a bookaholic; bookshops are my downfall. If I see a bookshop, that's it. I go in and I never come out again! It drives people a bit nutty.

Yesterday I went to Foyles in London and finally came out with four books. I thought, Now you've got to carry them home! Then I get home and I've already got them, which is even worse.

In the arcades in Southport there are some very old bookshops. There's one in particular that I go to all the time. It's got *everything* and it's full of interesting little corners. I walk around it full of wonder.

When I heard that we had Jane Russell coming on the show, I went to the shop and said to the owner, 'Here's one for you: Jane Russell!'

'I had her autobiography but someone bought it last week,' he said.

'I knew you'd have it!' I said. I'd missed it by a matter of days, it was such a shame. I love stories of old Hollywood glamour.

I don't know how many books I've got. It's just terrible. I can't seem to stop myself buying them. I can't believe I'm contributing to a book myself now, it's brilliant!

POCKET MONEY AND SAVING

JANE: I've always been a goody-two-shoes over money. I've always saved for a rainy day, but now I think money is for enjoying and I'm not frightened of it. Working-class people tend to have a fear of money. I don't know what it is but it's inbuilt in us. We think money rules us, but I've got to the point now where I have respect for money and I enjoy it.

COLEEN: One of the best things we ever did as a family was a film for *Tonight with Trevor McDonald* called 'Debt-Proofing Your Children'. The aim was to put an American woman's theory into practice to see if it worked. It was difficult at first, but it was amazing and it really worked, so we carried it on for four or five years.

It works like this: for a week beforehand, you write down

every single penny you spend on your children, including every time they ask for money, even if it's just fifty p.

At the end of the week you work out what you've spent on them, and it's scary to read, I can tell you! Then, instead of giving them money in dribs and drabs, you work out a budget for the month and give them the entire sum in cash.

Some people might say, 'I couldn't hand my kid a hundred and sixty pounds cash!'

'But you are,' I tell them. 'It's just that you don't realise it, because you're doing it in ten- and fifty-pence amounts.'

Every single thing they want after that, they have to buy out of their own money. So if you've cooked dinner and they say, 'Mum, I want a pizza,' you can say, okay, but they have to pay for it. And it's amazing how often they don't want a pizza in those circumstances. Obviously, if it's just that you don't want to cook and you order pizza for the family, then you pay for it.

Each month they have to save ten per cent in a bank account and donate ten per cent to a charity of their choice. They can do what they want with the rest, but they have to budget themselves because if they run out of money after two weeks, you can't give them any more.

It was difficult in the beginning. The boys' friends would ring up about going somewhere, but they couldn't go because they'd spent their monthly allowance. That was hard for me, because I'm so soft, but I didn't budge.

All of a sudden they stopped wanting football stickers; they didn't want designer shirts because they were paying for them. Within two months they had completely sorted it and they'd have money left over on the last day of the month. It really taught them about the value of money and they loved it because they felt they were being treated like grown-ups.

All the arguments about money in the house stopped. We went from, 'No, you're not having any more money,' or 'Stop giving them money!' to peace. It was amazing and it really worked.

SHERRIE: I've never been clever with money. If I had, I'd have bought a flat in London in 1969. I beat myself up about that. I'm sorry that I've never been clever with money, but I don't think it has ever mattered that much to me. Obviously, not having it is horrible.

I know people who live quite happily without much money, although I don't mean on the breadline. My brother, for instance, has always worked hard. He's got a restaurant and bar in Conwy. Money never seems to enter his head, yet he's one of the happiest people I know. I'm jealous of that, because I work myself to death and am always aware that I've got to earn. I have a phobia about earning enough and looking after my daughter and my grandson in the future.

My brother is right when he says, 'Sherrie, stop! As long as you can eat and pay your bills, and you're safe, and Keeley and Ollie are safe, that's all you need.'

Chapter 4

The Dating Game

Whether you're searching for love or happy flying solo, the exciting thing about the dating game is that you're only ever a heartbeat away from a head-spinning kiss that turns your knees to jelly. Especially if you're anything like Carol McGiffin was when she was single – she was never short of kisses! That woman has turned many a male knee to jelly in her time, the minx. But are you a good flirt and, if not, does it matter when you find the right man? Either way, Jane's guide to flirting will see you right and you can have lots of fun trying it out. (It works, it really, really does – trust us!)

In this chapter we'll be pondering the Big Questions about the hunt for love. Is there such a thing as an ideal man?

What should you wear on a first date? Has anyone ever had a good blind date? And is it important to spend time alone? Some of us have strong opinions when it comes to the singular subject of single life, so brace yourself. And be prepared for some toe-curlingly cringe-making stories too!

FLIRTING

JANE'S FIVE-POINT GUIDE TO FLIRTING

1. Spot someone you like, and if he likes you back, he will hold your gaze for more than five seconds. Be brave, and don't look away.

2. Then, when you see that he is holding your gaze, give him a smile. But not a fake one, a real one, because a smile is the most inviting thing for a man. (Oooh, hark at me, as if I know what I'm doing!)

3. The smile is usually the invite. If he approaches you, which he will if there's interest from both parties, be interested in what he has to say about his life. It's not all about you.

4. From then on, it's all in the eyes. You know they say that the eyes are the windows to your soul? Well, they are, and you can usually tell everything from them.

5. Start playing with your hair. That's always a dead giveaway. If he starts playing with his hair as well, you know you're in.

JACKIE: It's always very funny when we get a good-looking man on the show, because Coleen's a big old flirt, so she'll directly give them the eye or get a bit cosy with them.

COLEEN: Enrique Iglesias! Need I say more?

CAROL: We'd rather you didn't! Yes, Coleen, you're the flirting queen. But I'm hopeless at flirting. I can't do it and I never do it because I just don't know how to do it. I don't flirt with anybody. It's a running joke on the show. Coleen's always taking the piss out of me because she says I'm terrible at it.

I'm totally, totally oblivious to any attention from men. With me, the bloke has to make the first move and make it in an obvious way. It's not that I'm being hard to get or anything. I just don't notice it.

People are always saying to me, 'So-and-so fancies you.'

'I don't believe it,' I say and I genuinely don't believe them. I haven't got the radar on. I'm never looking.

I've been around this bloke I'm seeing for a long time and I'd never even noticed him. But when he started taking an interest in me, I became interested in him. I wish I had seen him before, but everything happens for a reason. The timing was right for then, so it's all right.

SHERRIE: Honestly, I've never been a flirt because I've never cared enough about men to flirt with them.

If I meet somebody I like, I'm nice but slightly overawed. I definitely can't flirt.

JACKIE: Don't you ever flutter your lashes even a little bit, Sherrie, or widen those big blue eyes?

SHERRIE: No, I don't think so. I'm sure I don't. Well, not really. Honestly? Um . . .

JACKIE: I thought so! What about you, Lynda?

LYNDA: I flirt with everybody, not just men. I don't like women who flirt with men as a means to an end, the kind of women who are incapable of having a normal conversation with a man without going all silly on them.

JACKIE: Like Coleen with Enrique? And Carol with Russell Brand?

LYNDA: Well, not exactly, but I can see what you're getting at! I have to admit that I like flirting. I think it's very healthy and it makes people feel good. Playing with double meanings and throwing something back and being suggestive in a jokey way puts people at ease and works a treat. It's so much subtler than lowering your voice an octave and saying, 'Darling, why don't you come up and see me sometime?'

WORST DATES/FIRST DATES

SHERRIE: When I was eighteen, I had a sort-of date with Steve McQueen. He came to my drama school to give a talk and I was chosen to take him around on a red London bus.

It was the date to end all dates! Later, he took me to a beautiful restaurant called the Poissonnerie.

Unfortunately I didn't realise that *poisson* means 'fish' – and I'm allergic to fish.

'I'll order,' he said. I was so nervous that I couldn't speak; in fact, I hardly spoke all day. The waiter put a plate of seafood in front of me and I politely ate the lot. But then I projectile-vomited all over Steve McQueen! I actually thought I was going to be Mrs Steve McQueen until that happened.

CAROL: Oh my god, Sherrie! What a wasted opportunity! You could have shagged him and all. Don't say you wouldn't have, because you would.

As for me, I don't really go on dates, not proper dates. I don't do dating. I've got friends who are serial daters: they're always going out with a bloke they hardly know. I think that's desperate behaviour. Dinner – eurgh! I don't want to sit opposite a stranger, eating!

JACKIE: I think the dating culture in the States is far healthier than it is in this country. When I was living there in my early thirties, I did quite a lot of dating. You're allowed to go out with different people and there's no sense of obligation, whereas in this country the lines all seem a bit blurred. Either way, I'm so glad I'm not dating any more.

Once my best friend Michael said, 'I know the perfect guy for you. You're going to get on like a house on fire!' So he set us up on a date.

When I met the guy, I couldn't believe that Michael had

done it to me. He was a long-haired, sandal-wearing, stoned-out-of-his-mind ageing spiritual guru-style hippy. I was aghast! I spent a pretty horrendous hour listening to him talk about his crystals and chakra lines over coffee, and then I got out of there.

'Do you know *who I am*?' I asked Michael later. 'What the hell were you thinking?'

'But he's so nice!' he protested.

That put me off blind dates forever!

ANDREA: I've not done any dating. My first husband and I were at a school together and met in geography. So we didn't do any dating. We just went out with friends to the pub. Then Steve and I met through work, so we didn't date either. Some people say I've missed out, but I don't mind. I wouldn't change anything.

CAROL: I say that I don't go on dates, but I've been on more dates than you have, Andrea! I suppose that the first time I went out with this boyfriend on my own was a date. It was only a sort-of date, because I'd seen him a couple of times before that, at parties, with other people.

It was quite funny, because I had just broken my toe, so I had to go out with a bloody great ski boot on my foot. There was no point dressing up because nothing looks good when you're wearing one shoe and a ski boot. So I was in jeans. I was probably very scruffy, but I don't think it mattered too much. I couldn't go far because I couldn't walk, so we went to the pub across the road, where we just sat and chatted. We had a really nice time and I thought, 'Ooh, I could get used to this.'

INTERNET DATING/SPEED DATING/BLIND DATES

CAROL: I would rather slit my own throat than go on an Internet date! Having said that, I joined an online dating site once, just to see what it was about. I would never have gone on any of the dates, though. I didn't use my real name; I put my name down as Davina McCall and I got so much mail!

At first I thought it was hilarious but it got on my nerves after a while. I just felt really sad for these people. I also felt guilty that they were wasting their time writing to me, so I closed it down. I was only a member for a month.

I'm so glad I don't feel the need for a companion – for love – to the point that I would go on the Internet and search for them. Each to their own, though. I know lots of people who have done it very successfully: they've met people through Internet dating and married them. But the process of searching for love seems a bit sad to me.

As for speed dating, I can't imagine anything worse! What's the point of going into a room and talking to someone for three minutes? It's not all that different to going to one of the bars in Bangkok and just picking someone off the stage. OK, money doesn't change hands at speed-dating venues, but it's a market. I might do it for research purposes if I was asked, but I wouldn't do it voluntarily.

SHERRIE: I haven't done any of that kind of dating, but I did go on a sort of blind date once. Well, it wasn't totally blind, because I'd known this boy when I was quite young. He was very, very handsome. Moving forward in time maybe fifteen or eighteen years, he rang me up, out of the blue. I don't know how he had my number.

'How are you?!!' I said in complete surprise.

'I'm fine. I'd love to meet up,' he said.

'I'd love to see you,' I said, thinking omigod, because he was just gorgeous!

'We probably won't know each other now,' he said. 'I know you because of your work, but you won't know me any more.'

'I will!' I said.

He suggested meeting at a restaurant. 'I'll stand outside the door and lean against the doorpost so that you can take a look at me first,' he said.

I thought, How amazing! I went and bought a new dress and everything.

I was sure that I'd be so overawed that I wouldn't be able to speak to him, because he was bound to be absolutely stunning, so I decided to creep up on him quietly. But when I turned the corner, I saw a little old bald man leaning on the doorpost.

Assuming that he hadn't arrived yet, I hung back and waited. Then the little old bald man looked at his watch and looked around him. He was obviously waiting for someone. Oh my god, it's him, I thought, and I ran away.

I didn't ring him afterwards and he never rang me again. Isn't that terrible? He must have guessed what had happened. He had once been so handsome, but I'd forgotten how short he was. I do feel bad about it, but then I also think it would have been wrong to go through with it when I already knew I wouldn't want to see him again. Some things are best left in the past, I think. Particularly beautiful boys!

HOW TO DRESS

CAROL: I wouldn't dress up too much on a first date. You don't want to make too much effort when you first see someone, because as time passes it will all taper off and they'll think, You don't make an effort any more!

SHERRIE: If it was someone like Jeff Bridges, who I love, I would be so scared that I wouldn't know how to dress. So I'd probably go in something like a black trouser suit. Even then, I'd be so jittery that I wouldn't be able to speak.

JANE: If I'm going out I'm usually suited and booted. I'm not a jeans type, although I wear them at home.

I wear a business suit on first dates because it's like an interview. I have a checklist in my mind, because I don't want to settle for second best, and I never do.

In the past, the girls were always on at me about someone or other, saying, 'Why don't you just go on a second date?'

'Because I know it's not going to work,' I said. I usually know by the first date whether it's going to work or not.

I go along with a businesslike attitude, but I'm still quite flirty. I think you can be very sexy in a business suit, because usually you've got stockings on. So, from his point of view, there is an element of, I wonder what she's got on under that? Although it looks very businesslike, imagination is a wonderful thing.

CAROL: I'm not sure about those checklists you do, Jane. You know: 'He's got to have this or do that.' I would never do that. You're creating such a job for yourself if you've got a checklist.

You always say, 'I'm not going to go out with anyone who's got this or done that.' How can you rule all those people out?

JANE: It's about compatibility, Carol, and standards. A woman has to have standards.

CAROL: No, Jane, a person is a person. I either like them or I don't. It doesn't matter what they do. Okay, I don't want to go out with a loser. I went out with an out-of-work actor once, who kind of took the piss, and I won't do that any more, because I've done it.

JANE: There you are, you see!

CAROL: Well, I'm definitely not going out with anyone who's out of work again. I wouldn't want to support someone. If I was going out with a bloke and he became unemployed, then that's different. But I'm certainly not going to get off with an unemployed actor again, no way. People have to work.

I'll know not to in future if the situation arises again. But as far as, 'He's got to be this; he's got to be that.' No, it doesn't bother me; I really don't care.

SAYING I LOVE YOU

CAROL: I don't think I've ever really been in love. I think I've still got it to look forward to. I've said 'I love you' in the past, but I probably didn't mean it, if I'm really honest. I probably only said it because they said it to me. So I'm sorry to those people I said it to! (Probably only two or three in my life.)

JANE: I don't find it easy to say I love you. I say it all the time to my mother, because that's a different love, that's absolutely unconditional. But with a man it's a big step to say I love you – and then god forbid if they don't love you back! I usually wait for them. They've usually said it to me first.

CHASING MEN – MAKING THE FIRST MOVE

JANE: I've not really chased a man, because a man will always come and chase you if he's interested. If he's not interested, there's plenty more out there. So I don't really go for one and think, I'm going to die if I don't get him! Men are like buses: it doesn't matter if you miss one because there's always another behind him.

JACKIE: In Jane's world, there's no need to chase men, or indeed buses, is there? How lucky you are!

I think that there's a difference between chasing and being open about the fact that you like somebody. Chasing smacks of desperation and men can sense that, so I don't think it's very appealing.

Equally, some of the nicest men are a bit clueless when it comes to noticing that a woman likes them, and they need a bit of a nudge. They probably appreciate being given some guidance as to what's going on!

LYNDA: I don't see the point in chasing a man. If they're not interested, they're not interested.

If somebody wanted to leave me, I don't think I'd have the chutzpah to say, 'Please don't leave me!' It would be more a case of, 'F*** off then.' What more can you do? You've got to think enough of yourself to say, 'Well, if you don't appreciate how wonderful I am, then there are plenty more out there who will.'

I accept the things I can't change and move on quite fast in my life. That's good and bad. When I've made mistakes, perhaps sometimes if I'd sat and given them a little thought, I wouldn't have gone and got into trouble the next time.

I don't have regrets. I don't allow myself to sit and think about it. I'd rather look to the next thing so I could say, 'I'm really pleased I did that,' rather than linger on regrets. Life really is too short.

CAROL: I've only ever gone out with people who have chased me. I've never really chased anybody. Wait, I did chase a pop star once, but I didn't go out with him; I just had sex with him. I was a groupie for a night. That was probably the only time. It was hilarious, the funniest thing I ever did.

He was in a band and they were playing in Folkestone. My sister and I went down to see them play. We booked into a B&B for the night and dropped our bags there, then trooped off to the venue. After the gig, we somehow managed to get backstage. We were so excited and it was such a laugh. Then she got off with the bass player and I got off with the singer. Result!

In the morning, my sister and I got up, went back to the B&B, paid for the room we hadn't slept in, picked up our stuff and went home. Everyone at work knew that I was a bit obsessed with this guy, so they couldn't believe that I'd actually got him and then run away. But that's what groupies are meant to do, isn't it? Leave without saying goodbye and run off with their mate, squealing with laughter?

CHASING MEN – PART TWO

CAROL: They come up with all these terms like 'phone phobia', but if he doesn't call, he's just not into you! Move on. Get another one.

JANE: Don't give him your number and then let him give you his: never both do it! Because then you're thinking, I'd better not ring him because he might ring me. So if one of you gives the number, that's great.

SHERRIE: I don't understand. You mean you don't give him your number if he gives you his number?

JANE: No, because if you're waiting for him to ring you and he's waiting for you to ring him, it gets confusing.

SHERRIE: So what do you say if he asks for your number? 'No, you're not getting my number, but I'm having yours!'

JANE: Just say, 'I'll take your number and give you a call.' Then take his number.

JACKIE: What do you do, Sherrie?

SHERRIE: I don't do much, really!

JACKIE: Do you give your number out to gentlemen?

SHERRIE: Sometimes I do.

CAROL: Yes, you'll find it on the walls of phone boxes . . .

SHERRIE: They don't ring me, though! I'm not very good at phones. You know when you think somebody's going to ring you and they don't ring you? Isn't that awful?
Occasionally, I've been the one avoiding calls, though. You know when you give your phone number to someone and they call you and you think, I don't want him to ring me *again*. Then they always ring you. The ones you don't want to ring always ring, and the ones you do never ring you!

JANE: What are you on about? If there's someone you don't want ringing you, say, 'Give us your number,' instead of giving him yours.

SHERRIE: When this guy rang once, I pretended I was foreign! 'You hav' zee wrong number,' I said, but then I realised that didn't make sense.

JACKIE: I think there's nothing wrong with ringing a man, just to give him a little nudge, if you are absolutely certain that you are both equally as interested in each other.

CAROL: The first night I met my boyfriend, he came back to my place. I don't mess about! But he didn't get my number and I didn't get his number.

JACKIE: Oh, he got your number all right.

SHERRIE: When did he leave?

CAROL: The next morning, but nothing happened! There was no number exchange at all and I'm not quite sure why. Another friend was there and he said, 'Aren't you going to get a number?' but I remember thinking, Well no, he knows where I am, because he works very close by.

So then I didn't know how to get hold of him and I thought he would be able to find my number. But three weeks later, it still hadn't happened. So I got his number off someone and texted him and said, 'Here you go, here's my number. Give us a call.'

I was sitting in the pub with my friend, waiting and looking at my phone. 'At least thirty seconds has passed,' I said. 'What's going on?' It took him about four or five minutes to text me back. So it was a goer, thank god.

JANE: Just a little bit like yourself! Wahay!

KISSING

CAROL: I love snogging. I snog everybody; I'm a terrible serial snogger.

SHERRIE: I'm not like you, Carol. I don't like kissing. It's too close. It's too in your face. Well I suppose it would be, wouldn't it?

CAROL: It doesn't have to be.

SHERRIE: Let's not go down there, please . . . What I'm trying to say is that I think kissing is sexy when he kisses your neck, and then he kisses your ears. If anybody kisses my ears, my legs go numb. It's just one of those things.

ANDREA: I can't bear it if someone kisses my ears. I lean back to avoid it and then I crick my neck.

SHERRIE: I love it! My legs go numb and I fall over, but maybe that's the point.

CAROL: I can't believe you don't like snogging. I just love it!

When I was single, I snogged strangers. I'd go up to someone and say, 'Come on, let's have a snog.'

SHERRIE: You did not!

CAROL: I did! I don't see the problem with it. I go out with my friends and we have competitions to see how many people we can snog. It's hilarious. Eleven in one night is my top score.

I like full-on snogging. Not slobbering, though. On competition nights it's best just to go for it, because it's only going to last a couple of seconds. Proper, full-on-tongues snog. Can't mess about. But if it's someone you quite like, then you might take a bit of time over it! I don't mind a tentative kisser. It depends who it is.

SHERRIE: Do you kiss the man who comes to check your gas meter, too, and taxi drivers?

CAROL: I have snogged taxi drivers before. There's nothing wrong with kissing a stranger, Sherrie. You should try it! It's fun.

COLEEN: I'm not sure about snogging in public, though. It has its place, but there are limits. I was sitting on a station platform and I saw this young couple walk up and I thought, Oh look at these two! One of them must be going back to university or something . . .

They walked down the platform really hugging each other. When they put the bags down, he put his arm round her and he kept kissing her. This went on for ages. Me, I was looking at them thinking, Oh, it's lovely!

He kept kissing her and I thought, Wow, he's so mad about her. They've obviously only just met.

But then the train pulled into the station and they both got on the train! And that really, really annoyed me and I wanted to go up and slap them and say, 'Can you get a room?'

The train was delayed and the journey dragged on for seven and a half hours. They sat in my carriage the whole way and all I could hear was snogging noises!

ROMANTIC GESTURES

CAROL: I've always said on the show that I don't like big romantic gestures. I once went out with a guy who took me to Paris. We stayed in a fantastic hotel. He put flowers everywhere and gave me lots of presents, but I found that it was all just a bit too much. I felt pressured.

But recently my boyfriend got me some flowers and I just think it was so sweet. I've still got them. I can't throw them away, even though they're all dead. The card is still sitting there. I should do something with them. I think I'm going to dry them.

So I don't usually like romantic gestures, but for some reason, when he does it, it's fine. And I don't usually like flowers, but I do now, because he sent them to me!

WHAT MAKES THE IDEAL MAN?

JACKIE: Ideal is different for everybody. You've got to think about what you want, what you're looking for and what works for you.

When the girls and I talk about our men at work, they're all very different. What works for me would in no way attract them, and vice versa.

I was in my late thirties when my husband and I got together. I'd been divorced and put the fairytale firmly to bed. I wasn't cynical, but I certainly didn't have any expectations of being married or having a family.

It sounds cheesy, but when I met my husband, I got the fairytale. David is, by a million miles, the best thing that's ever happened to me and as a result we've had these beautiful babies, Stanley and Florence. It still amazes me that I got this lucky, so I have to say that it's never too late!

CAROL: You're lucky that you're so happy. It means there's hope for everyone! But I don't think there is an ideal man, because nobody's perfect. Everyone's got bad habits and everyone's a bit annoying at times. We're human beings. We're flawed!

ANDREA: That's so true. We're not perfect but if, overall, you're good, understanding and good-humoured, you're getting there. What makes the ideal man? It's the same thing that makes an ideal woman really, just being a good person.

So why do women treat men like they're a foreign species? We're all human. Okay, men have a different take on things and women have a different take on things, but we're just people in the end. When you break it down like that, it's quite straightforward. Maybe women need to have more blokes for friends. Then they would calm down a little bit and realise that, yes, we are different, but not necessarily in a bad way.

CAROL: We're definitely different, and it's good that we're different, because life would be boring otherwise.

ANDREA: Okay, well you would never be friends with a woman who was horrible, would you? So why would you go on a date with a man who was horrible and then expect him to be nice to you?

I have met men that, the split second I've met them, I've thought, You're horrible! You might be handsome and smiling and buying us all drinks, but you're really mean, I can see it in you.

SHERRIE: You can't say what you really think about men if they are going out with your friends though.

ANDREA: Of course not. You would never say, 'Why are you with him?' But then a month later she'll tell you that he cheated on her or something else and you think, Well you can see it in him, so why did you think that he would be any different with you?

It's because they're looking at an idealised version of the bloke; they're seeing what they want to see rather than what's standing in front of them. They're ticking boxes and thinking,

I want a boyfriend, or, I want a life partner, instead of seeing what is actually physically there.

JANE: Is there such a thing as an ideal man? I don't think there is. I just think that sometimes we're blessed with meeting someone that we really get on well with. It has to be 'like' for me as well as 'love'. It's not just about love. Do I like this person, as well? I think that's so important. You've got to be compatible.

JACKIE: It's so true, Jane. You hear it all the time when you're young, with good reason, but you don't understand it fully until you're older, do you?

SHERRIE: There's a lot you don't grasp until you're older, isn't there? And in my case, some of it is still way out of reach!

HOW TO BE HAPPY AND SINGLE/ THE JOYS OF BEING SINGLE

JACKIE: When Carol was single, she didn't put on a brave face and sit at home lonely on a Saturday night. She had a great life; she was always off in some fabulous resort in some exotic country.

Carol is a girl about town. If I had remained single, I think she and I would be socialising quite a lot together, having a great time.

I truly believed that if the right person came along, she would open up her heart. And she has. She's glowing and full of the joys of life. It's fantastic to see.

CAROL: I'm enjoying myself, I must say. But it's weird having a boyfriend after so long. I was perfectly happy single – and I was always happy to protest that I was happy single. No one ever believes you, though. Now I've got a boyfriend, everyone thinks I was lying. 'Well done!' they say. Pat on the back. 'Brilliant, you've finally got a boyfriend!'

But I never wanted one. I wasn't looking for one. It's just that now I've got one, I'm very happy with the situation. However, I wouldn't be in this relationship if it weren't easy and right, because I'm not desperate. While I'm single, I love being single and I would be happy to be single again. So I don't need to be in a relationship.

I don't need it, but I'm absolutely loving being in it – at the moment. It feels lovely and natural, for the first time in a long time.

LYNDA: That's obvious for all to see. It's wonderful! You were quite wary of getting involved with someone, weren't you?

CAROL: Yes, because I know so many people in relationships who are not happy. It's hard work, as people always say. Well, it's quite hard work being happy single too, because you always have to prove it to people, or tell people that you are.

I love the freedom of being single. I really, really love sleeping in a double bed by myself. I love going on holiday alone and I love staying in hotels alone. It's nice to have someone to share it with, but I love doing it on my own.

I love to walk around my flat looking like a tramp; I love just leaving a mess if I want to leave a mess. It's nobody else's mess, after all. It's a happy state for me and I really do like it. Obviously, things aren't like that at the moment, because

I'm not single. But my boyfriend doesn't live with me. He's got his own flat.

I didn't always go out when I was single. Sometimes I sat at home of a weekend without speaking to a single person. I quite like the solitude and the silence and I like not having to speak to anyone for two days, because my job is talking. Instead, I read, watch a film, do a bit of writing and mess around with the computer. I love pottering and sorting things out. I love my sofa and sitting in on my own watching crap telly.

If you've been single for a while, you tend to walk around the house in the cosiest, comfiest stuff. I wear the same tracksuit bottoms and top every single day when I'm at home. But having a boyfriend snaps you out of that. I wouldn't dream of putting it on now. All my single slouchy clothes have been hidden in the cupboard.

JACKIE: When you were single, you always said, 'I'm really happy being single, but I'm open to the possibility of romance.' When it came along, you were open to it.

When Jane was single, she always said, 'I'm very happy single and I'm absolutely not interested, no way, never again!' Of course, you've got somebody now, Jane.

JANE: You go through different phases, don't you? I was very happy single, but then my new man came along . . .

DENISE: Ha! It hardly took Carol any time to start talking about her new bloke as her 'boyfriend'. I knew she would! It all rubbish – Carol and Jane McDonald – absolute rubbish!

CAROL: I can see why you'd think that, Denise, but—

DENISE: There's JANE: 'I'd rather have a cup of tea'; and CAROL: 'I don't want a boyfriend.' Nonsense! Then, as soon as they get one, they say, 'Ooh, I've got a boyfriend!' Don't get me wrong, I'm delighted for them – but I knew it!

CAROL: Well, what are you getting so worked up for then, Madam know-all!

JACKIE: I think a man could sweep Sherrie off her feet, even though Sherrie is more like Jane in that she says she's sworn off men for good.

SHERRIE: Maybe. I do get lonely and I'd love to meet somebody who I could really have a wonderful relationship with, but I never do. Jeff Bridges would be the man for me. I just think he is fabulous. Not only is he gorgeous, but he has that outgoing American quality that Englishmen often don't. Some Englishmen are too reserved, whereas American men just come out with it. They will tell you if they love you or they think you're wonderful. I also love Irishmen.

JACKIE: Sadly, not all American men are like Jeff Bridges, Sherrie.

COLEEN: And not all Irish men are like Liam Neeson . . . (sigh).

JACKIE: It's a real pity, that! Well, I got married very young the first time, so my single years were my early thirties, when

I was in LA. I really enjoyed being single. Having a good few years on my own was crucial to becoming a more rounded person. I don't think it does you any harm.

JANE: I was really, really happy being single for five years. Being single and staying single was the best thing I could have done, because when you come out of a marriage, you are so rock bottom. It takes time for you to heal and grow back into being the person you were before you were married.

CAROL: I totally agree with Jackie and Jane. So many of my friends have never been out of a relationship, but how can you be in one when you've never been out of one? If you don't learn to love yourself and your own company, I don't really see how you can form a proper relationship with somebody else. I know people can and do, but I don't see how.

People don't feel complete unless they're part of a couple, and I've never, ever felt like that. Ever. I never really wanted a boyfriend; I never wanted to get married. I know I did, but I never wanted to. It just wasn't something I was chasing after.

There are so many joys to being single. Everyone should try it at some stage. For me, being single means I'm never disappointed. It's a choice. I have chosen to be single in the past. It's not that I'm rejecting everybody, though. I've always said on the show that I've been open to something if it came along, but if it didn't, fine. People still don't believe it.

DENISE: What crap! You so wanted a boyfriend!

CAROL: NO. I. DIDN'T!

Chapter 5

Sex

If the scientific studies are to be believed, it's always on our minds. So although it's a bit of an embarrassing topic, we couldn't leave it out now, could we? Love it or leave it – and some of us do and some of us don't – it's an endlessly interesting subject. Since we girls happen to represent both ends of the scale, and everything in between too, this topic is always guaranteed to provoke debate!

Remember your first time? Of course you do! Everyone always does. Remember your second time? Thought not. Hang on, Carol thinks she does . . . actually, no she's not quite sure. Perhaps it was that time at Butlins? Maybe . . . So what's it like when you get to the ten thousandth time with the same person? How do you spice things up? And how do you stay interested when you've been up all night with the kids? What if you'd rather have a cuppa?

We don't promise to have the answers, but it doesn't really matter, nobody does. We'll always enjoy swapping saucy confessions. It's a core part of getting together with your mates, isn't it? So have a squawk and a gasp and a giggle along with us . . . how could you possibly resist?

HOW TO DO IT . . .

JANE: I didn't really come into my own until I was in my late thirties, which is when my confidence grew as a woman. I think good sex, great sex, comes from within. It's about what you find works for you, and having the confidence to go for that.

COLEEN: That's so right. Sex is very much trial and error. What you find pleasurable, someone else might not, so you need to learn about each other and be able to laugh when it all goes tits up.

CAROL: I once went out with a guy who didn't know how to do it, and I wasn't laughing, trust me. He was the first guy I'd been out with who was older than me. I couldn't believe that he'd got to fifty and didn't know what to do. How shall I put it? He was not really aware of how women work.

So I drew him a little picture. He took it fine; I'm sure he was grateful. I went on seeing him and he made vast improvements after that. A lot of his girlfriends since have probably benefited from my little lesson.

There's nothing wrong with telling someone what you like, or what you'd prefer them to do. I don't think anyone minds that. I would definitely draw a diagram again if I had to, because I couldn't stand not to say anything. What's the point in having sex, if they don't know what they're doing?

JANE: No point at all, love. Have a cup of tea and go to bed with a book instead . . .

Sex

DENISE: Do you remember how it was when you were young and you had no real idea of what you were doing? It was so hit and miss, wasn't it?

SHERRIE: Oh my god, yes. When I was at drama school, I didn't really even know what sex was. Still don't, actually! I've never understood it. I've always been quite naïve and used to fall in love with everybody I met. I was clueless.

I remember being at a party with a boy I was in love with. We went into a bathroom and he started to fondle me.

'Don't! What are you doing? Get off!' I said. I was thinking, Urgh, I don't like this, and I ran away. Sex just seemed like a lot of fumbling mess for nothing, and very little at the end of it.

Maybe I just haven't had good experiences. They say that when you're young you should meet an older man who will teach you things, and then you will go on to understand. Well, I never had any of that. I just had fumbling innocents.

LYNDA: I've heard from young men who say that young women don't want to hang out in a hotel room making passionate love all day. Can you believe it? Apparently, young women don't want to get messy. It's quite the opposite with older women, which is probably why younger men find them so attractive. 'Stay here, young man! You're not going anywhere . . .'

YOUR FIRST TIME

COLEEN: My first time was fabulous. It was all very romantic. He was my first love and I stayed with him for four years. I was very young though, at fifteen.

JANE: Fifteen? That is quite young. I was seventeen, which by today's standards is quite old. I've always done things by the book, so I made sure I had a proper boyfriend and I went out with him for a while. Our first time wasn't that brilliant, though. I was in a serious relationship and he was a lovely, lovely boy, but even at that time, I thought, Is that it?

It did get better, but I never thought, Come on, let's go and do it now! I was quite glad that I still lived with my mother and he lived with his.

COLEEN: I love the fact that my first time is such a great memory, because I meet so many girls who don't have that. Either they can't remember it or it was awful, but mine was lovely.

LYNDA: My first time was horrendous! I was a virgin when I went to drama school at nineteen but, because I'm an extrovert, some people assumed I'd had sex. Unbeknown to me, the second year were laying bets as to who would sleep with me first.

I went through the first two terms having the mickey taken out of me endlessly. So I decided that the best thing I could do was lose my virginity and get it out of the way.

I picked this bloke who was the prettiest boy in our year,

because it was a challenge to see if someone like me could pull the boy that only ever had pretty girls. I also knew that he very much kept himself to himself and wouldn't tell anybody. So I did it – and to be honest, I didn't realise it was happening. It was such a letdown.

Well, that was a waste of time! I thought. It kept me quiet for ages; I wasn't going to go down that route again, frankly. Then it all kicked off again a bit later. It was the 1960s, after all.

That experience has stayed with me all my life, I think. I generally get the sex out of the way quite soon and if it's no good I don't go any further. I like to get it out of the way because it's the thing I'm most suspicious of.

At the time I was very grown-up about it and went on the pill. I was determined that I would never get pregnant. It was a very responsible attitude, I thought, but when my mum and dad found out that I was on the pill, my mum wrote me a letter saying that they were very disappointed in me. I was very upset. Years later we discussed it and Mum admitted that she'd been wrong. Back then, times were changing faster than a lot of people could cope with, and it took her quite a while to catch up.

CAROL: My first time was behind the church at the local disco when I was fourteen. My friend had already done it and everyone in the school was fascinated. They all wanted to know, 'What happened?' and they wanted to do it as well.

It was like, Just get it out of the way! So I went behind the church, did it and probably never spoke to him again. It was 'orrible! It's always horrible, isn't it? How could it ever be nice?

I know lots of people who didn't do it until they were about eighteen or nineteen. What were they doing? I just couldn't wait. Why would you save it?

I was a terrible sex maniac when I was young, once I found out how to do it and how great it could be. I didn't do it again straight away, though. I felt too guilty. I felt really terrible, in fact, because I knew my mum would kill me if she found out about it.

I couldn't have coped if my mum had found out about it. I was staying at a friend's house that night and couldn't face her the next day, so I didn't go home for a few days. It was probably about a year before I did it again, with Pete at Butlins in Bognor Regis.

COLEEN: Bognor Regis? Was it worth waiting for?

CAROL: Not really, no. It was all over after one night.

COLEEN: Oh no!

DENISE: As for me, my first serious boyfriend was called Simon. He was my first love and I was with him from when I was fourteen to sixteen. It was a major relationship, but we didn't actually do the full business.

My first proper sex was with a boy who was two years above me at school. It was all right, quite good, except that it was at his dad's freezing-cold council house. I think I'd pretty much done everything else, so it wasn't like a huge deal. I'm still friends with my first boyfriends. They're all

married now too, and we've all been to each other's fiftieth birthday parties, which is really nice.

SHERRIE: That is nice. But do you ever wonder, what if? In another space, another time, I probably would have married my first lover. He was wonderful, a dancer called Freddie. I met him before I went to drama school, when I did musicals and shows all over the country.

Freddie was a natural ballet dancer. He went on to get into Royal Ballet School without any formal training, but he didn't stay there because Nureyev would never leave him alone. He was beautiful, blonde, with big blue eyes, and Nureyev ran after him all the time. In the end Freddie said, 'I can't do it!' He ran away and joined the army.

He came to see me at RADA, but I'd already met Bob Lindsay by then. I fell in love with Bob straight away, of course, because I was just eighteen. I didn't want Freddie any more, even though he'd given me an engagement ring. I'm afraid I sold the ring. How terrible of me!

SPICING IT UP

LYNDA: In a way, what's quite nice about long-term partnerships is that all that stuff about having to 'perform' is not there. There's an element to it that it should be like eating and sleeping. Have you flossed and had good sex today?

Equally, you've got to be aware that sex can get a bit everyday. What's exciting when you go out and meet people and flirt is that you're in a different place, out of your comfort zone. So if you don't want to get into dressing up and S&M – all of which takes time – just go somewhere different. Catch them on the hop!

DENISE: Like any man, my husband likes to be titillated. He likes nice underwear, but I get very lazy with my underwear. I'm not like Carol, who always has to have hers matching. It's funny: until last year, Carol always dressed for sex and didn't get any!

CAROL: Yes, very funny. I always wear nice, matching underwear. I'm absolutely obsessive about it.

DENISE: Yes, well at least someone gets to see it now! I know I could do more as regards the dressy-uppy side of things.

COLEEN: You should! I initially bought a nurse's outfit for a laugh. Then I mentioned it on *Loose Women*, which is the worst thing you can do. But in one way it was the worst thing and in another it was the best thing, because I've since had three outfits sent to me . . . for free!

Like most men, Ray loves the idea of me dressing up. I've got a nurse's outfit and a policewoman's uniform and a naughty housewife costume – I am a naughty housewife, anyway, because I don't clean the house enough! But obviously I don't walk around the house in dressing-up clothes, because I have children. Just the thought of them being in the cupboard is sometimes enough.

SEX WITH YOUR PARTNER

DENISE: I think you go through phases in a marriage. I'm actually quite relieved that Tim's sex drive seems to have balanced out a little bit, because he was always the more highly sexed of the two of us; ridiculously so, to the point that I felt almost harassed in my own home. I couldn't bend down to put a dish in the dishwasher without him seeing it as an invitation for a shag.

I used to feel under quite a lot of pressure, because I knew how important it was to him. It's important to me too, but a two-hour, child-free gap means something different to the man. He sees it as an opportunity for sex, while the woman is thinking, How much housework can I get done before the baby wakes up?

Tim used to equate sex with love, very strongly. If I wasn't gagging for it all the time, he would interpret it as meaning that I didn't love him. He knows now that isn't the case, so the fact that we go through phases of not having sex doesn't worry him on an emotional or ego level any more. Then we go through phases where it's much more regular. These days it's just a little bit more balanced and I don't feel the need to perform just to keep him happy.

There is nothing like that first knicker-ripping stage of a relationship, but there is also something nice about long-term sex. You can take your time, your partner knows what buttons to press and you're not having to put on a performance.

COLEEN: It always amazes me when people say, 'I don't mind him when he's drunk, because he doesn't want sex and falls asleep.' My husband's the opposite! It doesn't matter what time he has come in; it could be four or five in the morning and he might be bladdered, but the one thing he'll want is sex.

I always know, because he starts stroking my arm. Oh god, please! If I've been out with him, it's fair enough, but if I've been in bed for the last four hours and I've got to do the school run in a couple of hours' time, it's just annoying.

Either you've got to lie there and pretend to be asleep, or you've got to keep turning over and telling him to go away. Otherwise, you just let him and it goes on and on and on – because he's so drunk that nothing's happening – while you're lying there, thinking, Please hurry up and get it over with!

OUTDOOR SEX

COLEEN: Once I had sex in my back garden, but I've never done it in a field or anywhere like that. I quite like the idea of it, but it scares me too, because I'd be the one either to be caught or to end up in hospital with some horrible sting, having to explain how I got it.

JANE: Sex in the open air? No, I can't be bothered. If he can't afford a room, I'm not going.

ANDREA: I've been naughty in a car, and in different cars, too, and to my amazement, I owned up to this fact on the show. There was a section on the show about fast cars and I like fast cars, and suddenly I came out with this confession. It wasn't with lots of different people – it was with the same person – but even that was quite a big thing for me to admit. I'm a nice normal girl, really.

When I first joined *Loose Women*, I was scared of giving my opinions. I thought, My family are going to see this! Fast-forward to eighteen months later and the things I've confessed to on that show! You just forget you're on television.

PORN

COLEEN: A lot of women say, 'Well if he watches porn, it means he doesn't fancy me.'

But to me that's a load of rubbish. Porn is there to turn you both on, especially if you're watching it together. Ray and I have great fun watching it and I don't have a problem with that.

I think women especially should stop being so insecure about porn. They get very het up about it and see it as an absolute lack of respect. But sometimes men watch it just because they're men and they think about sex a lot. They get it over with, even if you're not there, and then it's done!

DENISE: I also think there's a place for the old Frankie Vaughan, as the people at work call it. A healthy interest in it is fine, but I know that some people's husbands are almost obsessed by it and go on their computer every spare minute of the day. I wouldn't like that. Tim's not very computer literate, but men almost always manage to find it, don't they?

Ages ago I saw a bit of a porn film that was made by women for women for the heterosexual market. It was very low budget, but it was very erotic. There's nothing less sexy than repetitive close-ups of sex – that's a man's thing. Boring! But this had a little bit of a story and the whole process was erotic. It still showed everything, but in a much sexier way. I loved it!

Ah, butter wouldn't melt! But which *Loose Women* did these little angels grow up to become? (Answers at the back of the book!)

Here are some of our favourite guests. Joan Collins is one classy lady.

And here's Coleen showing off her assets and flirting madly with Enrique Iglesias.

Blonde ambition. Debbie Harry is an absolute legend.

Nigel Havers – such a charmer!

Letting loose! From top left: Carol snogging Russell Brand; Sherrie preparing to terrify small children; the Loose Women girls spice up their lives; Carol tries her hand at pouting (or is she gurning?); Knowing Me, Knowing You . . . Jackie and Jane's tribute to Abba

From top left again: Jane and Carol try to break the world hula-hooping record . . . and fail; Carol snogs TV chef Gary Rhodes; Coleen thinks she's died and gone to heaven; Andrea takes it back to the streets with some gangsta rap; Carol kissing yet another unsuspecting male guest – this time it's Danny Dyer. He was hardly complaining though!

What cheek! Carol flashes at the Royal Television Society Awards.

And Denise reveals her Spanx pants.

Sherrie and Coleen before they got fed up of carrying the sandwich board round with them everywhere they went.

And here we all are – dolled up to the nines!

EMBARRASSING SEXUAL MOMENTS

COLEEN: There's always loads of embarrassment around sex when you come from a big family. I always think I'm really quiet, but apparently I'm not, because I'll come down in the morning and all my sisters are saying, 'Have a good time, did you?' They know what I've been doing and I don't like it!

SEX AFTER KIDS

COLEEN: It's difficult to have sex with kids in the house, especially teenagers.

JACKIE: Yes, they tend not to stay in their cots when you put them there!

COLEEN: Absolutely. I don't like it when they grow up.

CAROL: Jackie, how's it going? You're married, with two very young children . . .

JACKIE: I have to say that the body is willing at midday. The mind is still willing at six p.m., but come ten p.m., I'm just wiped out.

CAROL: So what you're saying is that you tease him all day: 'Ooh, darling, I can't wait,' but when you get to bed you say, 'No, I can't be bothered!' That's not very nice.

JACKIE: No, I don't think there are any complaints in that department, but it is a mammoth shock to the system to go from making babies to looking after babies! So you have to be crafty about managing your time. Leaving it until last thing at night is not a goer. Sometimes you have to forget dinner and go straight to dessert!!!

COLEEN: Why is he bothered if you're asleep while he's doing it? Ray's got used to it. I say, 'Don't wake me up, love. You don't normally, so . . . get on with it!'

YOUNGER MEN

LYNDA: Younger man–older woman is the right way round, because we last longer. Mr Spain is younger than me. He's fifty-three, but I'm sure he wouldn't mind me saying that he doesn't look like a toyboy; and I don't look much older than him, because I'm so fabulously gorgeous!

JANE: You are, love, ravishing. You're right, too. Younger men, yes! Every woman should have a younger man at some point. I've often said that they should be available on the NHS. I was very grateful to mine, because he brought sunshine back into my life after my divorce. He was the best tonic I could have ever had.

   He said, 'Stop getting so worked up about your problems! Just relax and have a laugh.' That young man made me relax, and that was because I knew he wasn't going to be a husband.

LYNDA: Exactly — it's great as long as you don't fall in love, because obviously that would end in tears, at some point. Still, it's in your control to turn this young man into the perfect lover and future husband for someone else.

SHERRIE: That's very generous of you! My husband was five years younger than me. But I always thought that was a mistake. I met him when he'd just turned twenty-one and you should never go near a man who's just turned twenty-one, because he's really only fifteen. You've got to wait until they're about thirty-five before they can even look at a woman properly, in my opinion.

I can't be bothered now, but if I could, I'd go for a slightly younger man. Men my age have all turned into strange people who want twenty-year-old flesh. They don't want a woman my age. So you have to go for slightly younger men who haven't reached that weird life-crisis stage yet.

COLEEN: Yes, but not too young! I appreciate younger men and I appreciate it if a younger man ever fancies me, but as far as a long-term relationship goes, I'm not into younger men. I mean younger, as in, twenty years younger. I wouldn't go near someone in his twenties, because I've got a son of twenty and I would feel a bit like I was going out with one of his mates.

Enrique Iglesias is just beautiful and *sooo* gorgeous. I couldn't take my eyes off him when he came on the show. But if I went out with him, it would make me feel old, and then I would have that battle with feeling the need to start having Botox, to warrant why he would be with me.

LIVING WITHOUT SEX

CAROL: I didn't mind living without sex. I think you just switch off. I actually found that my life was much less complicated without it, because it tends to cloud your thoughts and your judgement. You become, not obsessed . . . but distracted.

Now I am sexually active again, I can't believe I went seven years without it. But at the time you don't think about it. What you don't have, you don't miss. You get used to not doing it.

If a woman wants to have sex, it's very easy to get someone to do it with her. So in a way, I was choosing not to. I could have got off with someone if I'd wanted to, but I just didn't want to. I was quite happy not to do it.

Sex

My mum died in 2003 and everything switched off. When I came back to *Loose Women* in the summer of 2004, I couldn't even talk about sex. It was totally off my radar. I wasn't interested at all.

Something inside you dies when you lose someone you love – for a while, at least. My mum was the most important person in the world. She had such a massive influence on my life. She was the first person I really knew and loved who died.

I was probably quite lucky to get to forty-three without knowing anybody who had died. Luckily, time does heal. You learn to live with it. It took me about three years to wake up again.

One of my friends was the same. She's fifty now and her mum died about the same time as my mum, and she didn't have any relationships for three years. I don't think it's conscious. You don't even think about it. It just happens.

LYNDA: Grief takes many forms, and losing a parent can be the worst bereavement of all. It's so good to see that you've switched on again now, after going through such a tough time. And sex gives everyone a glow, so you don't want to go without it for too long.

SHERRIE: Living without sex doesn't bother me and I don't do any dating. I've lived on my own since 2001 and I couldn't have anybody living in my house now. That's it, no man!

JANE: For me, living without sex is very easy. It sounds awful, but I don't really bother with it. I don't have the urges like the other girls. I would rather have a good book and a cup of tea.

DENISE: Rubbish, rubbish, rubbish! All this, 'Ooh, I'd rather have a cup of tea,' is nonsense!

JANE: Denise, you're so wrong, because I wouldn't say it as often as I do if I didn't mean it. I really do believe there's more to life than that.

NO STRINGS SEX

COLEEN: I'm not into no-strings sex. I've tried it a couple of times just to see if I was into it and when it was over, I thought, Actually, I'm really not into that!

I think it's something to do with the idea that 'nice girls don't do that', which was drummed into me when I was young. We weren't practising Catholics, apart from my mum, but as a girl I was always told the same thing. It's probably still there subconsciously, so I always feel a bit like a slag.

I always think they're thinking, 'Dirty slapper!' even though nowadays it's all very liberal – and why not? Men do it; women do it; yet the worry is always there that he won't want to see you again if you sleep with him – for me, anyway.

Girls today don't have those worries, but actually I think they should, because I don't think things have changed very much. Boys are still the same as they always were.

JANE: I am very old-fashioned in my ways. I've really wanted to be like the others but I've never been highly sexually charged like they are. Sometimes I think that maybe I've missed out in life, maybe I've not been born with a certain gene. But it doesn't matter, does it?

I don't know what it is about me, but that's never the first thing on my agenda. More important is if I like the person, if there's a chemistry there and I get on with them. I'm glad in a way it comes across as old-fashioned, but in fact it's just that I've never had the urge that the others do.

Chapter 6

Long-term Relationships

Among all the weird and wonderful species in the world, humans are almost unique in staying faithful to one partner for any length of time. Are we the mad ones? Or is getting to your bronze or silver wedding anniversary actually worth the hassle of all those accumulated years of picking wet towels up off the floor?

In our relationships we've seen good times, bad times and moments of sheer awfulness, but most of us still believe in long-term happiness, with the right partner. So what are the answers to staying happy? How do you know he's the one? Can romance last? Does infidelity spell the end of a relationship? And will we ever get what we want by nagging? Here's where we get to grips with the challenges of monogamy and domesticity, not forgetting the 'downstairs loo' rule of course!

GETTING MARRIED

COLEEN: I've been married twice and both times it felt right, but different. The first time, I didn't for a moment think, I shouldn't be doing this! I was very much in love – we both were – and it was great. We eloped to Florida and we didn't tell anyone that we were going to get married, so we didn't have the big aisle moment and hundreds of family there, but it felt right and lovely and romantic.

The second time, with Ray, we did it properly at the church. It felt so different, because all our family and friends were there and I was older. I felt like a *woman* getting married – I'd been there and done it. I was a woman who had *lived*, instead of a young, excited girl loving the idea that, 'We haven't told our parents! Aren't we naughty?'

When you're younger, you have no cynicism. You just do it because you're in love and it's all romantic and lovely. But when I was older, it seemed like a much more solid, a much more grown-up decision. I wasn't getting married because of, 'Oooh, isn't this romantic and I get to wear a pretty dress for the day!' I was marrying for life, not just for the dress and the party.

I think that a lot of girls get so wrapped up in the big day that the anticlimax the next day must be horrendous. They're sitting there, thinking, Oh Christ, I'm stuck with him now: this is it!

ANDREA: I had a panic when we were flying off on honeymoon. Whoah, what have I done? I was really frightened about losing my identity. Then I thought, Well, I just won't take his name. After that it was all fine. It was just a three-second heart attack.

CAROL: I got married at Camden Registry Office. It was obsession more than love on my part, I think. It wasn't right and I knew it wasn't right, but I thought I could make it work and then it would be all right.

Despite everything, I believe in true love. Marriage is a sacred thing and commitment is really important. People don't think that way any more and they certainly don't expect it from me, but it's what I think. I'm quite old-fashioned like that.

DENISE: I knew it was wrong the first time I got married. I knew it as I was walking up the aisle. But I had a pair of blinkers on. I was so carried away by the fact that we looked lovely together that I bought into it. He was classically good-looking and I'd had my hair done beautifully!

We'd had a very volatile relationship, splitting up and getting back together. We were together for eight years and married for two and a half.

Tim was the complete antithesis of anybody that I'd ever been out with before, and it was the first relationship I'd had that had developed from being mates. It was a much slower burn, so it had a better grounding.

We had to get married in a registry office because I'd been married before. The church blessing came afterwards. The registry office was in Wood Green, and I wasn't too keen on the setting. I remember thinking, We'll go and do that because we have to, and the blessing will be where it all comes to light. Yet in fact I got quite emotional at the registry office, because I thought, This is how you're meant to feel on your wedding day! I suddenly knew how it was meant to feel, and so that day at the registry office was lovely in itself. It just felt right.

LYNDA: When I got married for the first time, I knew it was wrong, right from the start. The morning of my wedding, my father said, 'You don't have to go through with it.'

Knowing what it's like to be a parent now, I think it must have broken my father's heart to hear my reply.

'I kind of do, Dad,' I said, 'because I'm one of these people who has to give it a hundred and fifty per cent to know it's not going to work. If I don't do it now, I'll always wonder if it would have worked.'

People have a little voice that says, 'It's not for ever. I can always get out of it if it's a disaster.' What they don't understand is that it's very easy to get married, but it's incredibly difficult to get divorced, emotionally and financially. If you've got children, it's just a nightmare. If only people could be more aware of that, they wouldn't do it in the first place.

I knew it was a mistake getting married to my first husband, but with my second husband, who was Italian, I was absolutely passionately in love and it overruled any logic. So even if I'd taken a moment to think that it wasn't the most sensible coupling, I would have gone through with it anyway.

At the time, when I got married, I thought that any differences we had were cultural and so easy to solve. What I went on to learn was that it's probably quite rare for two completely different cultures to find a golden midway point. Somebody has to compromise. I also learned that a man has to be very secure in himself to deal with being married to an actress.

I knew it was completely right when I married Michael. I had never walked up the aisle until then. The first time I couldn't because he had been divorced; the second time I couldn't because I'd been divorced. I'm religious to a degree. I'm not fanatical, but I was brought up in the Church of England and I love to be part of that tradition. Michael knew that deep, deep down I'd love to get married in a church.

Things started to fall into place. I have a very good friend who is the Archdeacon of London, Peter Delaney, a remarkable man. He said that he could preside over the wedding. One of the churches he works in now is St Stephen, Walbrook, one of the oldest churches in London. Next to the Mansion House, it's a Christopher Wren church and a prototype for St Paul's.

I thought, Yes, I do want to get married in a church. But what about a white dress? You can't get married in a white dress at sixty. People will just laugh.

CAROL: Why? You could still be a virgin at sixty!

JANE: It would be a bit unlikely on your third marriage, wouldn't it?

LYNDA: My thinking exactly. So then, everybody else was going to be in black tie, and somebody said to me, 'Lynda, you've got to look different to everybody else in the room!'

You'd think as an actress I'd love that thought, but actually I'm not comfortable with lots of attention. We're back to that insecurity about putting yourself up as a sex symbol. 'No, but you must!' my friend said.

151

JANE: And your friend was right.

LYNDA: I hovered around it and the first attempt was a white dress with a long coat. The idea was that it would look like an evening dress when I took the coat off at the reception. Well, that wasn't working. Then I had a false start with another dress and a designer who wasn't very pleasant to me.

The wedding drew closer, and still no dress. A week before the wedding, we were on our way to the Gambia to relax and get a bit of a tan – still with no dress – when we stopped in London at a bridal shop. 'We can't go in there,' I said. 'It's embarrassing.'

We went in, and of course there was that wonderful moment when they said, 'Mother of the bride?'

JANE: They did not!

LYNDA: They did! 'No,' I said, and I went on to choose a dress that was just perfect. When I came back a week later from the Gambia, there it was. A full-on wedding dress!

Even though I was nervous, I so enjoyed the wedding service, because I was in this beautiful church I loved, the man who was marrying us was everything I'd ever wanted in a man of the church, it was in the round so I could see everybody's faces – and there was Michael. It was just perfect.

JACKIE: It can take a long time and you can make a lot of mistakes in the getting there, but I'm a bit of a romantic and I think that there's somebody out there for everyone.

CAROL: And you're the living proof of that statement, Jackie!

IS HE THE ONE? HOW DO YOU KNOW?

ANDREA: You don't necessarily know he's the one, but you know when you really like someone, when you're really attracted to them and when you love them passionately. There's a very big difference between loving someone and being in love with someone.

If you've been damaged before, then you'll always have doubts. The only time you have no doubts is when you don't know what it's like to be let down. You just have to enter a relationship with a lot of hope, I think!

STAYING HAPPY – THE ANSWERS

JACKIE: When I was younger, people always said, 'Compatibility is really important. Having a lot in common is crucial.'

As a youngster you think, How boring! But with age you realise that there's a lot of sense and truth to that. Being with somebody that you've got a lot in common with, having similar interests or backgrounds and being compatible

personalities are all hugely helpful in building a rock-solid foundation.

The ability to enjoy the simple little things in life helps too. If you're always looking for big highs, you're on to a loser. But if you both delight in everyday little things, especially if you have children and enjoy watching them grow, then if you're with the right person, it shouldn't be too much of an effort. It should be fairly easy. And of course fancying the pants off your husband is crucial – which I certainly do. And he makes me laugh a lot. And he doesn't seem to mind my appallingly mediocre cooking too much!

ANDREA: I agree with that! A feeling of ease between a couple is really important, because the answer to staying happy lies in talking, listening and laughing.

LYNDA: Absolutely, and if you're going to spend the rest of your life with someone, you have to live the same way. You need to like the same things, have the same attitude to life and relax in the same way. Opposites attract to a degree, yes. But the absolute practicalities of living together mean that I couldn't live with someone who was messy or untidy, with the best will in the world, and I couldn't live with someone who didn't love food and drink – although we've both given up the drink now.

DENISE: I always say that the marriage vows were invented when people died aged thirty-five. You were only meant to do ten years, max. No idiot would have suggested to people that it was supposed to go on this long!

LYNDA: A real test of our relationship presented itself when Michael came on the *Calendar Girls* tour with me. We were in each other's pockets every day. I hadn't experienced that for a very long time, if ever! We laugh a lot, so it worked out fine, although I had to tell him to shut up occasionally.

We couldn't get WiFi in Chichester and so he came into my dressing room and sat his bloody computer at one end of my dressing table while I was trying to have my quiet actor's moment. But he soon picked up on that; he's a very sensitive little flower. He now knows when to leave the dressing room and take a walk.

COLEEN: No one is happy 24/7. You are going to hit rocky patches or times when you're sad and think, This isn't going to work.

I think the key to it is always working together. It's amazing how much stronger you feel after each stage that you manage to work through together. That Ray and I got to the aisle was a battle in itself, because we'd had so much to overcome when we'd first met. So, when the wedding day eventually came, it was like, 'My god, we've come through all of that, we're here now and it was worth it! Now we know we can do it.'

DENISE: I have no better idea than anybody else about how to stay happy. We've had really hard times; we've had times when we've thought about going our separate ways and then we're not always glad that we haven't. We've always said that we wouldn't stay together just because of the children, but I think that having children makes you work harder at staying together.

My youngest is very used to us being apart, so the actual physical separation wouldn't be that apparent to him. For a lot of his life, Mummy has had a flat in Maidstone or Daddy's had a house in London, because of our work. He thinks we've got houses all over the globe! So really that side of it would almost be quite easy for him to adjust to.

That's what I mean when I say we don't stay for the children, but I'm glad that we have. I would find it quite hard to go and see Matty's band, or Louis in something at school, separately from Tim. There's something about the history and the bonds that I like. It makes for a very strong connection.

ROMANCE

COLEEN: If you want romance, don't marry someone like Ray! He's from Yorkshire! And he's a guitarist-muso type!

Seriously, if you're both romantic and you want it to last, it will last. People around you may tell you to get over it, but if you two are happy with it, then great.

I'm always being romantic. I'll go over and sit next to Ray on the couch and hold his hand.

'What are you doing?' he'll say.

'Holding your hand,' I say.

'Why?' he asks.

I think, I'm wasting my time! But I kind of like it too, because then I start laughing and we both end up laughing.

DENISE: There is a massive difference between falling in love and just loving somebody. I think you get a maximum of eighteen months of that stomach-churning stage, when you pretend you don't poo, you pretend that you don't fart and you still wee down the side of the bowl so that it doesn't make a noise when you go to the toilet. I loved that phase. I think that was another addiction of mine, really.

COLEEN: That initial feeling of butterflies in your stomach when you know he's about to walk in the room is wonderful, isn't it? But it goes after about a year. It's fabulous when you're thinking, God, I'm so nervous, I'm going to be seeing him tonight! But then it moves on to another level, which is equally as nice.

DENISE: That's right. I don't believe people when they say, 'I've been married thirty-six years and every time he walks into the room my tummy turns over.' I think that's complete and utter rubbish.

There are times in your marriage or a long relationship where you fall back in love with him, when he does something or he sings something, or you see him through other people's eyes and remember why you fell in love with him. It's nice when that happens, because you also go through periods where you could quite happily stab him.

Tim and I suffer a lot from not trying hard enough. It's difficult sometimes, because of the erratic nature of our jobs and our lifestyles. Sometimes, when I've got a lot of work on, I don't prioritise him as much as I should and then I realise that we need to reconnect a little bit.

ANDREA: Romance can definitely and absolutely last forever. My parents have been married for forty-three years and they still do romantic things. They buy each other little cards and say, 'I love you' all the time. They leave notes for each other, surprise each other and giggle like teenagers. You can hear them in their room, when they're staying with us. They giggle and giggle and giggle, and they're in their sixties.

Their relationship is very difficult to live up to. I felt like the biggest letdown in the world because I didn't live up to my parents' example. Don't get me wrong, sometimes I think they should do things slightly differently, but somehow they just work very well together.

HOUSE RULES – DOMESTICITY

DENISE: The 'downstairs loo' rule . . . Poogate, they called it at work, and it got more emails than nearly anything else.

We have four toilets in our house – three upstairs and one downstairs. The downstairs toilet is right by the front door, so it seems like common sense to me not to do a poo in it, because if someone then comes to the door it's embarrassing!! Okay, if we didn't have three toilets upstairs, but we do. So why can't my husband get it into his head?

Sometimes he tries to sneak in when I'm not looking and I say, 'How long is it going to take you to go upstairs and do a poo in one of the three toilets up there?'

ANDREA: Living with Steve is like learning to live with a great big dog. Of course, living with a great big dog is brilliant, because it adds a lot to your family. But you can't be as anal as you were before, because you'll just be shouting at the dog a lot and that's just going to ruin everybody's day.

So I'm much more laid back about tidiness than I used to be. Our bedroom and the study – places where nobody else goes – look like helicopters have landed in them. But I draw the line when it comes to the public rooms: I like the living room, kitchen and bathrooms to be really tidy. I must have clean, tidy bathrooms.

The one thing I cannot abide is wet towels on the bed! Why would you even think that's a good idea, for any length of time? Yet men don't notice wet towels on the bed, do they? I think they should get penalty points on their licence for leaving towels on the bed and the loo seat up. They'd have to make up for it . . . in other ways!!!

COLEEN: Yes, gardening! Seriously, I do all the usual tidying and shopping and school runs and stuff, but I'm not up at six in the morning to wash the kitchen floors. I'm not one of those people who has to have everything in its place or I'll have a nervous breakdown. I let Ciara have all her toys out all day and then when she goes to bed I put them away, no big deal. But I know people who don't let their children play in certain rooms and it's all a lot less relaxed.

JACKIE: I run a pretty loose ship. I was a single girl until quite recently and running a family house is quite a new experience for me, so it's still fairly hit-and-miss. I'm not a natural-born housekeeper, but I'm hoping that I'll evolve into one soon! My husband pitches in too, so it's very much a joint effort. He's about as good at DIY as I am at housekeeping; we're on a steep learning curve together, so neither one gets too impatient with the other.

SHERRIE: My daughter Keeley thinks I'm absolutely disgustingly untidy, whereas she is unbelievably tidy. It's frightening; she's just like my mother. She likes everything in its place. 'Why have you moved that?' she'll ask. I never know where anything is and she can't bear that.

She comes to my house and starts to iron. 'What are you doing?' I say. 'You've got a baby. Why don't you just sit down?'

'I can't leave it, Mum,' she says.

CAROL: Cor, does she want to come round my house too?

SHERRIE: No, Carol, I wouldn't have thought so. Your flat would probably give her a heart attack! I may be a bit untidy, but I'm a Virgo, and my Virgo side is quite picky. For instance, if I were cleaning the kitchen floor, every inch of it would have to be scrubbed. I can throw things down and just leave things around, but if I decide to clear up, I'm meticulous.

CAROL: You sound as if you're saying you never clean the kitchen floor.

SHERRIE: I don't at the moment, actually, because I'm never there. But when I do, I do it thoroughly. It's definitely a mania. Take my garden: I haven't mowed the lawn for ages because I've hardly been at home, but when I do get round to mowing it, that lawn will have to be cut within an inch of its life and I'd have to do every corner with scissors. So I've got a craziness in me . . .

JANE: Oh no, love, life's too short to cut the lawn with scissors!

SHERRIE: Yet my lawn's about knee-high now and that doesn't bother me. It's a case of total extremes, which drives me a bit crazy, because I think, Why don't you just cut the lawn? No, but it has to be cut straight, in lines, and I won't let anybody else cut my lawn. I don't know what that's all about! I don't know who I get it from.

My mother has a big apartment filled with lots of ornaments and everything is perfectly placed. I don't have ornaments, although I do have a six-foot Buddha. Mostly I have big wide spaces with nothing there, and it drives my mother crazy. 'Why don't I get you some dried flowers?' she'll say. But I won't have dried flowers. I'll only have real flowers. So we're absolute opposites.

I've got big white settees, the ones with the big backs, and a great big glass coffee table covered in candles, because I've got a thing about candles. I have to have candles lit all the time – otherwise my brain addles, because I have an insane life. I find them very soothing and calming.

JANE: Do you feel happy when you get home and kick off your shoes and sit on your sofa, love? Like I do?

SHERRIE: As long as the right number of candles are burning, yes I do!

NAGGING VERSUS ASKING

JACKIE: I think there's an art form to trying to get your partner to do something like household chores. It doesn't work if you tell someone in a nagging tone; you'll probably get a lot further if you suggest that it 'might be nice if . . .'

My husband is very good at doing things if he remembers, because he isn't at all lazy but he is a bit absent-minded, so he doesn't remember very often. I'll ask nicely quite a few times and then, if all else fails, it'll be a Post-it note on the front door saying, 'Don't forget to take the bins out!'

INFIDELITY – HOW TO GET OVER IT

COLEEN: It's important not to make any rash decisions; try and not make decisions based on pride. Obviously it's very hurtful when you find out that your partner's been unfaithful and it really knocks your confidence, but it might be worthwhile accepting that maybe you could have done some things better, but didn't. But don't blame yourself!

After that, just get happy, because they hate it when you get happy, they bloody hate it when you get over them!

It took me two years finally to say, 'Actually, do you know what? I don't love you any more. Go away!' In those two years, I kept taking him back and believing all the tears and the letters and I-love-yous. The flowers kept turning up, but he kept letting me down. Then, one day, two years later, I just woke up and thought, I don't love him now. It was a great feeling, a very powerful feeling.

DENISE: We've had major ups and downs. Neither of us has been the best behaved of people. I tend to take the rap for it: the press shows more of an interest in what I do than what Tim does, because of my soapy background.

That is why, when my affair became public knowledge, Tim never really spoke out against it. It was me what's done it, your honour, but we both had to take responsibility for why it happened.

It sounds like I'm condoning it and I'm not; it sounds like we have that kind of marriage and we don't; but we agree that a sexual infidelity is not the worst thing that Tim could do to me. There are far worse things that he could do or be to me than a one-night stand somewhere. Coleen and I are on the same side about this and the other girls aren't.

I'm not saying that I'd be overjoyed about it, but some people say, 'That would be it, that would be the end,' and I'm sorry, but I'm too realistic to have that view. I don't want people to think that I'm advocating open marriage, but I think that monogamy is very, very hard. I find it very hard and I think that people who don't find it hard are usually lying, or nobody ever asks them. It's very easy to say, 'I never would,' if you never get the chance!

I just don't think there is any real need to tell. Men often have that drive to off-load their guilt and therefore purge themselves of their sins. Then it becomes a case of: 'What's the problem? I've admitted it, haven't I?'

As I've said before, If you fall in love with someone, then obviously tell me, but if you have a one-night stand, don't tell me. Why would you want to tell me? If it doesn't mean anything, then don't tell me.

SHERRIE: I'm not so sure. I was married for a long time and the first seven years of my marriage were fine, but the rest was a disaster. I didn't come out of the breakup well at all. In fact, I came out of it very badly. It wasn't losing the person that I couldn't get over, it was what the person had done to me: the dishonesty and all the lies. I felt I'd been stupid in not seeing it and I had this awful sense that I had lived with somebody I thought I knew, but in fact I had no idea who this man was.

So the pain and upset was nothing to do with losing him. I now know I should have walked away when he had his first affair, which I kind of knew about at the time and later forgave. I forgave it because I felt that, since I couldn't do anything about it once it had happened, I'd better just carry on. But I should have left earlier. I know I should have left.

JACKIE: Infidelity would absolutely be a deal-breaker for me. Hopefully you're with someone with whom you share common values, but if one of you changes drastically, then it's really tough to keep it together. Above all, I know myself too well. The loss of trust following deceit would change me and how I behaved in the relationship. One of you would be a guilt-ridden cheat and one of you would be a mistrusting open wound, and then the two of you would no longer resemble who you were when you found this amazing magic together. I suppose you could live together without the magic, but forever is a long time to be disappointed.

JEALOUSY

COLEEN: I've now worked out that a lot of men are jealous over you because of what they're doing, or what they know they're capable of doing. So they assume that you're doing the same thing, or are capable of it.

Initially, when I was young, I used to think when men got jealous, He's behaving like that because he's mad about me and can't bear the thought of me going off with someone. I tried to turn it into a positive, but it wears you down in the end. You stop going out because you can't be bothered with the hassle of him phoning and saying, 'Who are you with? Are you with a man?'

Eventually, you stop pandering to it because you realise, This is stupid. If you do pander to it, the man will still carry on and have a life and flirt and do all of those things, but your life stops. Then you lose your friends and your personality and all of a sudden you are a stay-at-home mum. That's all you do. Ultimately, I think the man is quite happy with that, because he knows where you are.

But eventually you think, No, sod it! It's his problem, not mine. Usually, as soon as you stop pandering to them, they become a lot better.

Chapter 7

Holidays & Travel

We all need a break every now and then, but are holidays all they're cracked up to be? From first-love blues at Butlins, make-or-break getaways with lovers, terrible hangovers after one-too-many dodgy pina coladas, or nightmare flights with hyperactive kids, in our experience travel can actually be quite stressful! Or, as Sherrie once found, in Cyprus, downright life-threatening!

But nothing is ever going to stop us packing our bags with a new horizon in mind and a song in our heart, is it? Whether we're loading up the car with bulky kids' stuff, neatly rolling outfits to pack in our cabin-only luggage, or skipping alongside an overloaded porter as he strains under the weight of five matching suitcases, holidays are one of our biggest indulgences. They give us some of our most vivid memories, and we'll always count down the days to our next big escape.

HOLIDAY ROMANCES

CAROL: In 1974, when I was fourteen, I went to Butlins in Bognor Regis with my friend and her parents. It was a brilliant holiday. I was growing up and finding out about boys and it was my first time away from home.

One night I got off with a guy called Pete, who looked like David Bowie. I was with him for one night only, though, because he dumped me the next day! I was completely heartbroken. What made it worse was that my friend was going out with his friend and she carried on seeing him for the rest of the holiday.

The day I got dumped, I ended up sitting by the swimming pool, crying my eyes out, while my friend was off with the other bloke. Then, 'What Becomes of the Brokenhearted?' by Jimmy Ruffin started playing, which made me cry more. I was mad about Pete. Back home, I got hold of some Indian ink and a needle and tattooed a 'P' under my watch.

About twenty years later, I was in Folkestone with my sister and I had it covered over with a butterfly. It doesn't actually look like a butterfly, it just looks like a blob, so it's still there to remind me.

SHERRIE: Oh dear. You probably don't want to remember that, do you?

CAROL: I don't mind. It's all part of growing up, isn't it?

ANDREA: I've only ever had one holiday romance. It was in Wales with a Spanish boy I met on an Outward Bound course trip with the school when I was sixteen. He taught me how to snog. All we did was snog furiously in the games room. He was really good. Well, I thought he was good, but I didn't have much to compare him with. I never saw him again after that holiday.

I had only ever snogged one person before that and he was terrible. Even with my lack of experience, I knew that it wasn't how it should be done. Oh my god! I remember opening my eyes and thinking, This can't be right! It just went on for ages.

CAROL: I've had quite a few holiday romances, actually. I nearly married a Greek boy when I was twenty-four. I met him on holiday in Corfu and I went back to Greece to marry him – I packed in my job and everything. At the time I was working in the secretarial pool of an office service centre that offered temporary office space.

He came for me in a speedboat and we went to his home on the mainland. Suddenly, in the middle of the night, I panicked: I got up, packed my stuff and ran away. I got on the ferry to Corfu and went back to my friend's – and then I had to hide all the time because he kept coming over to try and find me. That was a lucky escape.

SHERRIE: I fall in love all the time. I once had a holiday romance in Cyprus. I was going to marry him, but he was quite a bit older. I was twenty-one and I think he was thirty-two, which seemed very old to me. When you're twenty-one, everybody looks ancient, don't they?

He wanted to marry me: he more or less gave me a flat in Famagusta. I even went to meet his mother and father. Although it would probably have been the wrong thing to do, I might have married him, but then in 1974 Turkey invaded the island – there'd been years of violence between the Greek Cypriots and the Turks and Turkey was trying to stop the island being annexed to Greece.

At the time, my grandmother and I were at the RAF base in Limassol with my cousin, who was in the RAF. I remember lying on the floor with machine guns going off everywhere and my cousin screaming at me, 'Keep still! Stay down! Don't move from the floor!'

As the machine-gun fire battered against the metal shutters of the windows, I kept still as long as I could. Then everything went quiet. We went on waiting and waiting for what seemed like an age. Finally, they got us in a Jeep that took us to the military airport, where we were bundled on a plane home.

A lot of my Greek Cypriot friends were murdered and their houses taken during the Turkish invasion. My boyfriend managed to get out and make it to Larnaca, but his beautiful Weimaraner dog was killed. Later, it was a relief to hear that he was alive, along with his mother, because a lot of the people I knew had been killed. I never went back to Cyprus, but I did hear from him again a couple of times. The last thing I heard was that he had got married and become the Mayor of Larnaca.

JANE: Does that mean you could have been Mayoress of Larnaca?

SHERRIE: I suppose so. Imagine that!

JANE: Well, you would have had to learn the lingo, for starters.

SHERRIE: Oh dear, I'm not sure how I would have got on, because it's all Greek to me!

CAROL: Nice one, Sherrie! I haven't had a holiday romance for a long time, but when I was in my twenties, I had some kind of romance every time I went on holiday. It just made the trip more interesting and fun. Me and my friends used to think, Where can we go where we can get off with boys? Wherever we went, that's what we did. Then, in my thirties, I got bored with it and stopped.

HOLIDAYS AS DEAL-BREAKERS FOR RELATIONSHIPS

JACKIE: Holidays can be deal-breakers in relationships. It's a long time to spend with someone if it's not going to work, although it's never happened to me, personally. Actually, my husband and I went away together for the first time and came back married, so I guess you could say that it was a very successful holiday.

TYPES OF HOLIDAY

JACKIE: These days a holiday has to be child-friendly with limited stress and things that the kids enjoy doing. If they are happy and having a great time, then we all have a great time.

In my single days I was quite adventurous, though. I went camping in the Amazon, to Palestine for a week, to Colombia and Mozambique. I would never do that now. Your priorities change when you have children, although when they're a lot older, I would like to take them off the beaten track and expose them to different cultures. I'd hate them to grow up with a narrow view of the world.

SHERRIE: Unlike you, Jackie, I discovered the joy of travelling quite late. My husband would never go on holiday. He would never go anywhere; he thought it was a waste of time. But these days I've got the travelling bug. I love it! I do talks on cruise ships and in the last four years, I've been everywhere, from the Caribbean to Russia. It thrills me to go to places I've never been before.

I found Russia fascinating, especially the Summer Palace in St Petersburg. It's the most extraordinary place. They're spending millions restoring it. There's a gold-leaf room that was destroyed and they've rebuilt and redecorated it, in gold leaf. But then you go into St Petersburg and you see little shops with Crimplene dresses in them – and I think, What is that all about? They're spending millions on gold leaf when they haven't got any money, and the shops are full of Crimplene dresses.

I said to a Russian woman, 'Do you not think that all the money they're spending on the palace should be spent on the people?'

'No, no!' she said. 'Our wages go to the palace. We rebuild the palace before we do anything else.'

I found it very strange.

JANE: I like a good cruise, me.

CAROL: Funny that!

JANE: I go on holiday with my mother at least once a year because, although I live with her, I don't see her a great deal.

I'm always down in London doing concerts and we don't have as much quality time together as I would like, so we nip off and have a cruise every now and again.

She is really good fun to be with. We'll sit there with a glass of something or a cup of tea, watching people and saying, 'Did you see that? What's going on there?' We share the same sense of humour, which helps. We giggle like mad.

LYNDA: I love going to hot places, but there's always one drawback.

SHERRIE: What's that?

LYNDA: Mosquitoes!

SHERRIE: Oh no! They terrify me, too!

LYNDA: You're lying on the beach or by the pool and the tan is coming along a treat and you hear a buzz and you think, Don't you dare bite me!

SHERRIE: But they always do, don't they?

CAROL: Mosquitoes don't bother me all that much, actually. I go to Asia three or four times a year, and there are loads of them there. I go to other places during the rest of the year as well, but at Christmas I go to Singapore, then on to Bangkok, and then I go to Phuket in Thailand for three weeks. Same place, every time. All the same people go, so it's like a big family, with all these different couples and their kids. It's nice to have a ritual at Christmas.

I haven't really got a big family any more, and now my

mum's gone, there's no reason to stay in England for a family Christmas. I see my brother in Singapore, so that's kind of family. Anyway, I just don't think it's that important. Christmas is just another day, really.

JACKIE: You don't really buy into the whole Christmas thing, do you?

CAROL: Not really – I suppose I'm a bit of a Bah! Humbug! Scrooge kind of person. I'd rather be away, because it's so manic here at Christmas. Everyone goes mad with all the shopping and the commercial side of it.

COLEEN: I can't bear going away. I've only ever been out of this country once at Christmas. It was the only Christmas we ever worked and we went to Indonesia. I absolutely hated it, because when I got up on Christmas Day, it was a boiling ninety degrees and not at all Christmassy.

CAROL: Except to the Indonesians!

COLEEN: Well, it just didn't feel like Christmas to me, and Christmas dinner was rice and chicken in a sauce. I thought, Where's my turkey? I didn't like it.

JACKIE: I'm with you. I spent quite a few Christmases away when I lived in the States. Obviously it was warm in California, and I used to comfort myself by going to this shopping centre in downtown Hollywood called the Grove. They had fake cold wind blowing down the streets and every twenty minutes there was a snowfall parade—

COLEEN: I love that!

JACKIE: And people going round dressed in Dickens costumes
. . .

CAROL: Outside air conditioning? That's really good for global warming, isn't it?

COLEEN: Well, so is flying to wherever you fly to!

CAROL: But I'm not the only one. There's something like three hundred people on that plane.

COLEEN: Well, she's not the only one walking through the Grove with air conditioning.

JACKIE: I don't do it any more! But I used to miss that whole British eat-too-much, watch-the-telly . . .

JANE: . . . full bottle of Baileys . . .

CAROL: Oh no!

JANE: Because I'm a singer, I work every Christmas Eve and Christmas Day, New Year's Eve and New Year's Day, and that's always been my life. I try to take my family with me when I go. They come kicking and screaming, 'We don't want to go with you!'
   I say, 'You're coming, that's it.'

JACKIE: Would you ever say no to the work? Would you ever say, 'No, that's it! I don't care how much they throw at me. I'm going to stay at home and watch the telly?'

JANE: No, because then I'd end up cooking for all the people that came to our house, and I'd rather go somewhere else and have someone cook for me!

CAROL: That whole family thing, where you sit there and eat too much and drink too much is awful! By the end of it you can't actually get up. You have to stay horizontal because you've eaten too much . . .

JACKIE: With the top button on your trousers undone, because you're so full . . . lovely!

CAROL: All that indulgence and excess, it's so uncomfortable! Everybody eats all day because they're bored.

COLEEN: Do you not eat a lot or drink a lot when you're over in Thailand, then?

CAROL: Well, I might have some noodles!

COLEEN: And five beers!

JANE: Nothing tastes finer than bread sauce and cranberry sauce with a bit of turkey, though.

COLEEN: And so say all of us, except Carol!

WEEKEND BREAKS

CAROL: I've been to Bangkok for a long weekend quite a few times. Bangkok is fantastic; I love it. It's my favourite city in the whole world. There's just something about it . . . the energy, the chaos, the smell, the people, the nightlife and the hotels. I love it all.

It's relatively cheap, compared to London, and flights are cheap, and the timing is good for the flights. You can go on a Thursday night and come back overnight on a Sunday night. That means you get there on Friday afternoon, so you have Friday, Saturday and all day Sunday. You fly back at midnight on Sunday night and you get in to Heathrow at six a.m. on Monday morning, in time to go to work. It's easily do-able.

I know everyone thinks I'm totally nuts, but I've done it four or five times. Getting on a plane, going to sleep for nine hours and waking up in a completely different city and culture on the other side of the world is just the best thing to do. I don't understand why more people don't do it.

People make such a great fuss over long-distance travel, but it's not difficult really. Even if you have to travel economy, it's not that bad. Some airlines have lots of legroom, so it's perfectly spacious and you're just going to go to sleep anyway. You can have a few drinks, or maybe take a sleeping tablet, and wake up having had a lovely night's sleep. (Also, if the plane crashes, you won't know anything about it!)

SHERRIE: I never worry about things like that. I love flying. I only wish I did it more.

CAROL: I have about twelve or thirteen holidays a year.

JANE: Blimey, Carol, it's a wonder we ever see you!

CAROL: Well, I like to go to different cities and look around. There aren't many places I haven't been to. Last year I went to Doha in Qatar, which was really interesting, because I'd never been to a Middle Eastern country before.

I go sightseeing in new places, but I don't need to sightsee in the cities I go to regularly, like Paris, because I've been so many times. I've done it all in Paris and New York; I've done it all in Bangkok and I don't need to see anything else there. I just get there, go to the hotel and sit by the pool outside. That's it, that's all we do. I don't know exactly what it is about it, but I just love being there.

I write travelogues about where I've been. I don't do it for work, because if I'm getting paid for it, it turns the holiday into a job. So I do it like a diary, like a journal.

I hate blogs and I hate bloggers! I hate people who think everybody's interested in everything they're doing. I don't care! I don't think everybody's going to be interested in what I'm doing either. No, it's just for me. I go back and read what I've written and think, Wow! That was brilliant, wasn't it? It's amazing what you forget.

I'm just a mad photographer and I've got thousands and thousands of photographs. Downstairs at home I've got four shelves full of photo albums and there are loads more on my computer. I spend an awful lot of time distracting myself, just picking up an album and looking through it. I love it, because it reminds me of certain times in my life.

KIDS ON HOLIDAY – PLANES, AIRPORTS

ANDREA: I think they should have children-friendly planes for families only, so that parents can relax and know their kids are not going to annoy everybody.

For me, ninety-nine per cent of the stress of travelling stems from my fear that it's going to be awful because the children will kick off. I set out thinking, This is going to be really terrible; it's going to be a nightmare.

If I just chilled out, it would probably be fine, but I can't help myself. It's because I don't like fuss. My kids can scream and yell as much as they like at home, but I don't want them disturbing other people. You know, kicking the seat in front, throwing things and doing what toddlers do. I can't bear it. I don't even like it when I'm with friends who talk too loudly and people turn round and say, 'Shhhhh!'

So if they could invent family-only planes where all hell could break loose and no one would care, I think they would do very well. It would be so great to know that they're going to have nappies and milk on the plane, or colouring books, and the air stewardesses aren't going to look at you like you're something they've trodden in because your child is screaming and refuses to sit down.

The worst time I ever had on a plane was with Finlay. He was two and we flew to Africa to see my parents, who were living there at the time. I was travelling on my own with him and for some reason, he went absolutely hyper, through the roof. I think it was a reaction to something he ate.

For ten long hours he screamed, kicked the seat in front, head-butted the seat behind and attacked me, pulling my hair. It wasn't normal behaviour; he just went mad. At one point he wriggled out of my grasp, pooed himself and ran past me into first class with poo running down his leg. I could see everybody staring at us, which is my worst fear; I hate that feeling of people tut-tutting at me. Argh!

What do I do? I wondered. Do I open the curtain and say, 'I'm so sorry, he's mine'? Do I just stand and wait, or do I run after him? Somebody must have grabbed him, because within seconds a stewardess came out of first class with him and threw him back at me. The stewardesses were horrible to me for the

rest of the flight and by the time we got to Africa, I was in tears.

If they'd been helpful and nice to me, it would have made the situation so much better. I'm sure they'd recognised who I was and thought, Typical telly person with a nightmare child! But it wasn't like I was sitting there sipping wine, reading my book and letting him get on with it. No, I brought out toys and all his favourite things to try and calm him down and make him happy. Nothing worked, though. I would have to say that was one of my worst experiences ever. It was really hideous!

CAROL: I'm not at all keen on Heathrow Airport! It's chaotic and old-fashioned. I think it's absolutely outrageous that a country like Great Britain should have such low standards at one of its main airports. It's the first place that a lot of people see when they come to this country. But it's a necessary evil – I have to go there to get out of the place.

My favourite airport is Singapore Airport. It's one of the busiest airports in the world but I've never had to queue at immigration, not ever. I've probably been in and out of Singapore twenty or thirty times and I've never had to queue or wait for a bag. It's so perfectly planned that it never feels busy, and yet at Heathrow you can't move.

I also love Luton Airport. I often fly easyJet around Europe and I go out of Luton when I can.

SHERRIE: Luton, Heathrow, wherever – I love being at airports and I love flying. I used to go to the airport just for the experience of being there, but these days I feel a bit cheated when I come away and I haven't gone anywhere.

PACKING A SUITCASE – HOW TO DO IT

JANE: When I go away, I take everything that I could possibly want. I pack for England and you can't lift my case. I do a lot of cruising, where you need to get dressed up a lot. So you need the right jewellery, the gowns and the bikinis.

I always take: white and black sandals; stilettos; a pair of gold or pewter shoes, so they'll go with anything brown. I also need certain bags, because I have to mix and match, and I never like to be in a situation where I haven't got the right jewellery to go with the right outfit.

I'm a professional packer, so I roll everything up. All my outfits are planned in advance and I would always wear a certain necklace with a certain dress. I test everything out on a clothing rail first. I learned that off my sister actually. She said, 'Just put it all out on your rail and think, that's Monday, Tuesday, Wednesday . . .' That's how I do it now. It helps, because I've got so many clothes, it's ridiculous. Everything is colour-coordinated in my wardrobes. I'm a bit OCD about my clothes.

CAROL: I've had to perfect my packing because of all the restrictions on airlines. I only carry hand baggage, because I can't be doing messing about at airports.

I'm now brilliant at packing. I'm the best packer, because I've done it so many times. I don't iron anything, ever. Even when I get there I don't iron anything. Instead, I buy certain things for travelling, which don't crease, and I always take the same things. I've got a holiday drawer at home, so I just take stuff out of the holiday drawer and put it in the case.

I can't remember the last time I went anywhere cold. Paris can be cold but I usually only go for three nights, so I don't need much. Obviously if I was going skiing I'd have to take a big case, but I haven't been skiing for about three years.

JACKIE: Now that I travel between London and Scotland every week, I've got packing down to a fine art. I always keep it to hand luggage.

I do very well with the kids' stuff too if we are going to stay with other family members, which we do a lot. I've got spare prams, nappies, baby wipes and clothing at my parents' house and my inlaws' place, and the grandparents have their own stashes of toys, so I can take the bare minimum. But if we go away to a hotel, we pack a ridiculous-sized bag that's actually a flight bag for a double buggy and it is full to bursting – you could seriously stash a couple of bodies in there and nobody would be any the wiser. How do such small people need so much big stuff?

ANDREA: Suitcases fill up quickly when you've got kids, but I'm pretty good at packing for myself. I only take what I need. I always have a suitcase ready, because I sometimes get sent away at the last minute for GMTV. I get a call in the afternoon: 'Right, you're heading to Scarborough,' and I have to be prepared to leave within minutes. So I always have a bag full of stuff, ready to go: toothpaste and shampoo, a hairdryer, an extra phone charger, etc.

When I was twenty-two, I backpacked around the world for a year. I set off with so much stuff: curling tongs, about twenty pairs of knickers, three towels (one for my hair, one

for my body and one for the beach).
After three days in India I realised
what a mistake I'd made and got rid
of it all. Ever since then I've made
sure I don't over-pack.

LEARNING TO DRIVE

ANDREA: My dad taught me to drive when I was seventeen.
He was phenomenally patient, considering how bad I was. I
had the normal jittery nerves that plague learner drivers. Every
time a car came along I swerved into the kerb and I couldn't
change gear without looking down. My dad taught me enough
so that I only needed a few lessons with a proper instructor
to get me through my test, and I passed first time.

JANE: My brother and an ex-boyfriend taught me how to drive.
Everybody had a go, really. I also saved up for driving lessons,
which my mum and dad couldn't afford to buy for me.

CAROL: This is a good test of how old you are. How much
were your driving lessons?

JANE: They were about five pounds.

CAROL: Mine were three pounds. I think they're about thirty
to forty pounds now.

JANE: Per lesson? Oh my goodness, cost of living's gone up, hasn't it?

CAROL: Did you pass first time?

JANE: Well, no. During my first driving test, a bus driver pulled right out in front of me and I called him something. Then I turned to the examiner and said, 'Did you see that?' He just drew a line right through my test sheet. Forget it! I passed the next time, though, and my first car was a gold Vauxhall Viva.

ANDREA: My, how flash!

Chapter 8

Winning Battles

Sometimes life can be very tough. Some challenges are so difficult to overcome that at times it seems they'll defeat us. We have all been through hard times, both physically and emotionally, times when we were convinced we wouldn't get through the tunnel, but we did – we came out the other side. And when you face your own battles in life, remember that you will get through them too. Here are some of the struggles we've encountered. We hope you find them comforting and inspiring.

WHEN THE GOING GETS TOUGH

LYNDA: During the ten years I was on my own, I nearly went down the cracks. All that sitting in the kitchen with friends and copious bottles of wine, getting fatter and more bitter. Bitterness and regret are very unattractive.

When I was working I was fine. The worst thing was dealing with unemployment; not having anything to do was a killer. When the boys were little, my days were always full and I'd organise my work around school hours. But now they were getting older and didn't need me so much, I had a lot of free time when I wasn't working.

One night I had a bit of a run-in with a friend when we were drunk. Sometimes when I drank I used to stand outside myself – perhaps it was the '*in vino veritas*' effect – and I looked at myself and this other woman and I thought, This is so depressing, sitting here slagging everybody off. All we could say was, 'The world is terrible and look what it's done to us! It's not our fault.'

CAROL: I agree, sometimes when the wrong mix of women get together and have too much to drink it can get a bit bitter and depressing.

LYNDA: Well yes, and just like that, I decided, No, I'm not going to have any of this. I'm going to keep my head together.

This realisation coincided with a job, fortunately. It was an episode of *At Home with the Braithwaites*, which was great, because it meant getting into work mode, going up to Leeds and filming up there. In an instant, I dropped that whole way of life.

It's interesting how, if you're in the wrong group of women at the wrong time, what they're doing is compounding the felony. Actually, you need people *not* to indulge you and I think you need to be aware of that. I have lots of friends who have gone through divorces or illness at this point in their lives, and yes, it's great to have friends and it's great to rally round. But you've got to keep an eye on what's beyond.

I started exercising in 1999 and I've been doing it ever since. There have been gaps – I can't do it when I'm on tour

– but having that discipline and making myself get up, even if I'm out of work, has worked wonders.

This sounds awfully 'goody', but I also started doing quite a lot of work for charity. I'd go and do the odd thing that other people probably didn't feel like doing, like opening a charity shop in Huddersfield, or visiting a home. A: it means you have to get up and get dressed and put your makeup on, and B: it reminds you of exactly what's going on outside in the world.

I've got a couple of friends who are struggling to fill their time in the out-of-work periods at the moment. Since they're not the kind of people who would join a society, I'm thinking about saying to them, 'Why don't you volunteer for something?' I know they're going to look at me as if I'm off my rocker, but never mind.

The trouble with this business – whether you're in acting, makeup, stage management or costume design – is that you, with the best will in the world, think it's the centre of the universe. That's the only way it works for a lot of people. When you're in it, you're entirely consumed by it, so when you're not in it, you're lost. The energy level, everything, is lost.

So it makes sense to replace it with another kind of energy. Getting out there and seeing people is one way. I know it sounds trite, but to see people struggling with illness or disability really puts things in perspective. You think to yourself, I'd better shut up.

Five years ago, when I was fifty-five, my career hit the desert. Suddenly the jobs didn't seem to be there in any shape or form. Casting people said, 'You don't look fifty-five.' I wasn't sure if they wanted me to come back looking like a grey-haired old lady. I was desperate to play Miss Marple types, but I couldn't play them because I didn't look old enough. It's all very well looking younger when you're thirty, but it's no good to anybody when you're older! The irony was that I had been told that I wouldn't work until I was forty!

What am I going to do if it has all finished? I thought. What can I do if I've not got a job as an actress? One of my very good friends is a makeup girl and it's the same for makeup girls: directors want gorgeous, pretty women doing makeup, even if they can't do the job as well.

My friend had a sister with an apartment on the Costa Blanca, so we decided to go there and see what was on offer. The plan was that we would both buy something that we could potter about in if there was no work. After all, we'd rather be old in a hot country than a cold country.

I was still drinking then. 'We can go on drinking and people will just think we've got dementia,' I said. Off we trotted.

There was this amazing little community of six villas around the pool. They were only little, two-up, two-downs, and my friend bought one. Two doors down there was a tiny little apartment. 'I'll get this, then,' I said. It was a mile from the sea and within walking distance of the town, which was perfect, because she couldn't drive (and although I could, I might not be around, or too pissed). That night we went out to celebrate.

We were rather hungover the next morning, and I had my mouth round a very large English breakfast, when somebody in the café said, 'You should speak to Michael Pattermore about your mortgage.'

'Get him in here!' I said.

He arrived, and there he was, bless him. We've always laughed about the first time we met: if he could bother to speak to me again after what I looked like that morning . . .

Anyway, he did get us our mortgages, which was absolutely brilliant, and I did my actressy thing and said, 'If you're ever in England, do call in, darling!'

And he did. He came round for dinner one night and never left! We've never looked back. I didn't even spend one night in my little cupboard flat, because Michael had a villa and I went there instead. It was bliss.

ANDREA: Ah, we all love a happy ending! Especially since you've been through so much. You've had some hard times too, haven't you, Denise?

DENISE: Yes, probably the biggest battle I've faced in life has been with depression. It started as postnatal depression, but it wasn't like I had it and it went away. It opened up a tendency to clinical depression in me, which continues to this day.

It took me completely by surprise. I didn't have a history of mental illness. I desperately wanted a baby. I was madly in love with Tim. We had money in the bank. Everybody was excited about the upcoming birth. There were no outside factors to cause depression.

I had Matthew privately. I was going to go National Health, but the local NHS hospital was a grim, depressing, Jack-the-Ripper kind of place and they kept losing my notes. I felt I couldn't have my baby there if I had the choice, so I went private, without realising that the private hospital I chose was a natural birth hospital.

'I want to know that pain relief will be available if I want it,' I said.

'Of course it will be available, Mrs Healy. We're not living in Victorian times.'

I had a thirty-six-hour labour and although they did give me pain relief eventually, it was a traumatic birth.

Eventually it was all fine. Apparently, I was the only mum who didn't anxiously pull the call cord at night. I wasn't anxious, which can sometimes induce panic attacks. Even when I gave birth I wasn't anxious, although I had a hell of a long labour. Looking back, I think it was too long.

JANE: It sounds it.

COLEEN: You poor thing, Den. That must have been so exhausting.

DENISE: Matthew was fine, though. He was perfect, in fact. Tim and I instantly fell in love with him. I had him on the Saturday and on the Wednesday I took him home. As we were driving back from the hospital, I said to my husband Tim, 'I feel really weird, as if I'm outside looking in.'

I went on to experience the baby blues for the next twenty-four hours. Everyone gets it: you sob over every card you open. I expected it and I was prepared for it, but I wasn't prepared for what happened on the Thursday night.

Just after I'd gone to bed, I had a panic attack for the first time in my life. It just came from nowhere, *from nowhere.* You know when you nearly crash in a car and your heart pumps and races? Eventually you calm down and the feeling goes away. But that Thursday night the feeling didn't go away. Every time Matthew made the slightest noise, my heart raced faster. I was terrified, because I had no idea what was causing it.

In the morning, after hardly any sleep, my boobs had gone from Jayne Mansfield boobs to nothing. The whole lactation process had stopped overnight. I had no milk. My tits were totally floppy.

The midwife came round. 'Oh my god, that's really unusual!' she said. 'I don't normally see that.' It was the last thing I wanted or needed to hear. My heart started racing again. 'I've only seen it happen when a bereavement occurs, when someone loses a spouse or the child,' she added. 'Yes, that's very interesting. Well, you'll just have to go out and get him some bottles.'

My parents arrived the next day to see their first grandchild. I wasn't feeling right, but nevertheless Mum and I took the baby out for his first walk. As we sat having a coffee, I said to Mum, 'I feel like I'm in a dream situation.'

'You don't feel depressed, do you?' Mum said. Being a psychiatric nurse, she was alert to signs of depression.

'No, I just feel really weird,' I said.

Oh dear, my mum thought. We started to walk the half-mile back home. On the way, I went into a newsagent's and heard about the Hillsborough disaster on the news. It was 15 April 1989.

I came out of the shop and said to Mum, 'There's ninety-six people been killed at this Hillsborough disaster.'

'Oh God, that's terrible!' she said.

When we got home, Mum asked me a question about it. 'That was a dream!' I said to her. 'I told you I dreamt about that disaster.'

'Darling, you told me about it as you came out of that shop just now,' she said.

'Stop trying to make me go mad!' I protested. 'I told you that it was a dream.'

At that, Mum knew the writing was on the wall. Within half an hour of getting back to the flat, I was looking at Matthew as though I didn't know who he was.

This black, black, blackness crept up on me, and within no time at all I was feeling suicidal. I don't remember what happened next, but Mum found me trying to climb out of the window of the flat.

COLEEN: Oh my god, how awful for you, Den. It sounds totally uncontrollable.

DENISE: It was! And it was all so sudden. Tim had gone out in the morning, saying, 'Bye darling, I'm just going off to play golf with your dad.' When he came back, there were medics round my bed.

COLEEN: How horrific, for both of you. Your parents must have been out of their minds with worry, too.

DENISE: They were. What made it worse was that a lot of people didn't recognise postnatal depression as a serious condition. My mother took me to a GP who said, 'I had six children, dear, and I didn't have time to get depressed.' Can you imagine?

She was saying this to someone who had just tried to throw herself out of her bedroom window, someone who had been a normal, functioning person two days previously. I tell you, my mother would stab that GP if she met her again!

I came across this outdated attitude a few times, always from older people. In their day, postnatal depression didn't have a name but, if you think about it, we've all heard someone whisper, 'Auntie Muriel went a bit funny after the birth.' I remember my granny saying it about someone she knew. Of course, it went untreated back then.

For years my mum worked as a psychiatric nurse at a hospital for people with mental disabilities. She knows that there were people there who had been admitted for postnatal depression and then became institutionalised because of lack of treatment. It really upsets me to think of the women who had my illness in an earlier generation.

My mum had to take unpaid leave from work to help me out, because I just couldn't function. I became trapped in a cycle, because I was so frightened of my illness that I could just bring it on myself. My fear of it would bring it on. I stopped doing theatre because of the fear of getting a panic attack whilst on stage, which did happen. I knew it wasn't stage fright because I had done theatre for years before I ever did television. No, it was my depression.

The depression became progressively worse over the next few years. My periods of being well were shrinking and the severity of the bouts was intensifying. I wish that I had been able to speak to someone openly about it. When you're poorly you need somebody to say, 'I was there and I'm better now.'

JANE: There's so much more information out there now, too.

DENISE: Yes, but although there have been huge advances in awareness since I first became depressed, it's still taboo and there is still a stigma attached. People who don't understand it say, 'Pull yourself together,' or 'Snap out of it,' or 'Go and buy a new dress!'

COLEEN: I can't believe anyone said that!

DENISE: They did! So many people didn't understand. Then, about four years ago, I'd just finished doing a series called *Down to Earth* and I was very up and down. It had been a really awful time because I had admitted publicly that I'd had an affair. It was a horrible time for us as a family, so I'd been really wobbly. However, I dealt with situations like that as an emotionally traumatised person, not as a depressed person. It was the same when my mum had cancer – I was emotionally traumatised by it, but not clinically depressed.

I went on to do a pantomime at Stockport. It wasn't exactly a stretching role and I was only really doing it because it was up the road from where I live. I was absolutely fine in rehearsals. Then, on the first day we opened, they let me go off for the afternoon to the *Manchester Evening News* Theatre Awards, where I won Best Actress. It was fantastic, really lovely, especially as my mum and dad were there because they had been given a tip-off that I'd won.

But then I got this ridiculous idea into my head that, because I'd won this award, everybody would have really high expectations of me in the pantomime. I became convinced that I would be rubbish. My depression came rushing back and I opened the show severely depressed. It was just horrendous.

Things went from bad to worse. I was vomiting before I went on stage and I barely ate for two and a half weeks, because I can't eat when I'm depressed. I can eat when I'm fed up in a normal way, but my appetite goes when I'm clinically depressed.

We had lots of young kids in the pantomime and I didn't want them to see the state that I was in, so the only person who knew about it was my dresser. I got steadily worse, until one day something in me broke. Unbeknown to me, my dresser phoned Tim at the interval. When he arrived, I had collapsed on the floor of the dressing room and lost all sense of where I was. I insisted on going on to finish the show, but afterwards Tim went upstairs and told the director, 'I'm really sorry, but you're not going to be seeing her again.'

JANE: What a hero!

DENISE: Yes, I slag Tim off as part of my act, I suppose, and we've had our major ups and downs in the twenty years we've been together. But the one thing I can't fault him on is his support of my illness. From day one he never ever doubted that it was an illness, even though he'd had no experience of it or anything like it.

He met this woman who was a flirty-flirty-wine-fag woman and very quickly I got pregnant, which we were thrilled about. But within a year I was a different person and he had lost me. It was very, very hard, but he never, ever doubted that it was an illness. When I get poorly, the people I need are Tim and my mum. I become almost childlike in my need for them.

JANE: What was the reaction to you pulling out of the panto?

DENISE: The kids in the cast accepted it straightaway and most of the press were moderately sympathetic to the fact that I'd had a breakdown. But one local paper really upset me. The girl playing Snow White had broken her wrist, so she had a plaster cast on, and the paper put something like, 'Denise Welch let down her fans by pulling out of the show, citing "nervous exhaustion", whereas her brave co-star battled on regardless of her broken wrist.'

I tried not to let it upset me, but it did. What they didn't realise was that I would have gone on and done that pantomime if I'd had a cast from head to toe. I've done many shows with a sick bucket in the wings.

JANE: That is so unfair! How did you get better, love?

DENISE: Two years ago this June, I was up and about again, but I just wasn't well and not eating. I hated the fact that I was worrying my parents all the time, especially because Mum is in fragile health after suffering from cancer. They know when I'm not well; they can hear it in my voice.

Honestly, I wasn't sure if I could go on feeling like that for the rest of my life. I would never do anything dangerous because of my children, but I longed to take a pill and have it all go away. I was so sick of battling it.

I had heard about a doctor in Baltimore and was on the point of going to America to see him when I got talking to a friend of mine who recommended a London specialist called Professor John Studd, so I rang him. The memory is so vivid: it was 22 June 2007, and I was in the corridor at work at *Waterloo Road*.

'My name is Denise Welch and I'd really like to come down and see Professor Studd,' I said to his lovely secretary.

'He'll make you better,' she said – and he has. It makes me want to cry even to think about it.

It turned out that the depression might have been caused by a hormonal imbalance. I was almost completely lacking in oestrogen. 'No wonder you've been the way that you have,' the professor said. 'People have been known to commit murder because of a lack of oestrogen. You're completely and utterly impaired.'

He was so straightforward about everything. Then he asked what my sex life was like. 'To be honest,' I said, 'I have no libido whatsoever. Mind, I have been married nearly twenty years!'

We chatted a bit about this and it all made perfect sense to him. He put me on Oestrogel, which is oestrogen in gel form.

'What about the anti-depressant I'm on?' I asked. 'It's quite low dose. Will they counter the effect of the treatment you've giving me?' He said they wouldn't. So I still take anti-depressants and, at the moment, the combination is working.

I still always talk about my illness in the present tense; I still live and deal with mental illness, but it hasn't come back since I first started to see the professor. I feel like I'm testing it all the time. There are certain situations, like hangovers, worry or lack of sleep, that would always trigger it. There was a time when I would have found it difficult to talk freely about it, because I'd think that I was bringing it on by talking about it. But now, for the first time in twenty years, I'm not frightened of my illness. I feel normal.

Depression robs you of your feelings. I used to explain to people who didn't understand it that if somebody had come to my door when I was depressed and they'd said that I'd won seventeen million pounds on the lottery, or that my family had been wiped out in an aircraft disaster, I would have felt nothing either way.

I'm a huge advocate of anti-depressants, of medication used correctly. Like my mum used to say, 'If you've got bronchitis, you think nothing of taking an antibiotic.' But people with depression feel bad about being on pills. I would get to a period of wellness and say, 'Right, I'm coming off those pills,' and my mum would always try to dissuade me.

They won't help if your boyfriend has split up with you, because no matter how emotionally upset you are, that is a normal reaction. Grief is a normal reaction. Anti-depressants help with clinical depression because there is a certain chemical missing, and they redress the imbalance. They get grouped with happy pills and tranquillisers but they're nothing like them. They simply enable you to see the light at the end of the tunnel. I'm so grateful they exist.

JACKIE: You've really been through it, Den. But what's so great is that you've come out the other side. You've survived!

DENISE: Yes, it's amazing, isn't it? Touch wood!

JANE: Well done, love. You've done really well getting through all of that.

DENISE: Thanks, love.

JACKIE: And Sherrie, you've been through tough times, too, haven't you? I know you were very affected by your father's death.

SHERRIE: Yes, as many of us know, it's very hard when a parent dies. Carol had a hard time when her mum died, and I miss my dad every day. He died aged seventy-six and every day of my life I speak to him. I wish he hadn't left me. The day he died, I opened the door to a journalist by mistake. He pushed a microphone right in my face and asked me about my dad.

'Can you put that away?' I said. It was the only time I ever refused to speak to the press.

'Oh, sorry, Sherrie,' he said, and then he pulled the most enormous bunch of flowers from behind his back.

'If you'd done that first, I wouldn't have been so cross,' I said. I think it was the only time I said an angry word to a journalist.

It was very, very hot that summer. I sat with my father in his coffin at the funeral parlour for two weeks, because I found it hard to let him go. I just sat and talked to him, day in, day out. He would have laughed because I was in *Coronation Street* at the time and there were hordes of photographers outside, even though Granada did everything they could to make them leave me alone. It was absolute madness.

The days passed, but I wouldn't let the funeral company take him away. They began to broach the subject gently. 'Miss Hewson could we take him?'

'No, leave him with me!' I protested.

Then the next day I looked at my father and realised that he had gone completely. So I said, 'It's okay, you can take him now.'

'Thank you,' the funeral director said, 'because he couldn't have hung on much longer.'

As I was leaving I took one last look at my father and said goodbye.

JANE: Oh love I'm so sorry, it must have been awful.

SHERRIE: Well, I don't think you ever get over losing someone you love, it doesn't really fade and you don't forget. You just learn to live with the grief, or around it. You get through it any way you can. I think about it a lot of course and some days I do get upset, but mostly I think about all the many happy memories I have of him. I'm lucky that he was such a wonderful man.

Chapter 9

Breaking Up Is Hard To Do

We have all gone through the pain of a broken relationship –
and we probably wouldn't be the people we are now if we hadn't
experienced heartbreak. But that doesn't make it any easier to
deal with, of course. Breaking up with a partner can be
completely agonising, and some days you just don't know how
you'll get through it.

So it's good to know that you will make it through to the
other side. We know, because we've been there . . . and survived.

HOW DO YOU KNOW IT'S OVER?

COLEEN: I wasn't blind when my first marriage was coming to an end, but it took a while to notice the build-up, because it started with lots of small things. His behaviour and attitude towards me gradually changed. I know now that he was seeing someone else, but I didn't realise that at the time. There were little signs at first − they slowly began to creep up on me until I began to suspect that he must be seeing someone.

He was always finding something else to do before he came home. He didn't seem bothered about what I did any more. He was fine about me going on holiday with my sister, which immediately made me think, There's something not right here. Before, all hell would break loose if I had suggested something like that but now I could go away for a week without him?

I thought, He's not bothered! So I started to test him. 'Me and the girls are going on a hen night . . .' I said.

'Great, you'll have a right laugh! See you when you get back,' he said.

A hen night! He knew there was going to be all kinds going on, but he was happy for me to go. I remember saying to my friends, 'He's up to something, because he's just not bothered.'

So those were big signs for me. Plus, we weren't making each other laugh any more. At least, he wasn't laughing any more at the things that I knew used to make him laugh.

ANDREA: That must have been so hard for you, Coleen, especially since you are so funny and everyone finds you funny.

COLEEN: It's just awful when the laughter goes out of the relationship. Suddenly you're getting on their nerves more, and little things that you've always done are irritating them, or they don't notice you exist.

One day, my first husband came home with a friend. Whereas normally he would walk in and I'd be the first person he'd try and find, this time it was forty or fifty minutes before he came to say hello to me in the lounge, and that was only because his friend said, 'Where's Coleen, by the way?'

'Oh yeah, where is she?' he said. I went to bed and cried my eyes out that night because it had taken him all that time to realise I wasn't there.

LYNDA: That must have been very difficult. It sounds like a really tough time.

COLEEN: Yes it was horrible. I'm so glad it's behind me now.

JANE: You get this gut feeling, don't you? You can tell when you don't make someone happy any more. Plus, you can tell there's something wrong when you don't feel happy going home.

LYNDA: There's not much you can do about it, either. I couldn't save my first or second marriages. Acting out my desire to please was the wrong thing to do, culturally and psychologically. What I've learned is that there's a standard that I now have, that I'm secure with, and if people don't reach that standard, there's really not a lot of point in trying to make them come up to it. I won't be horrible to them or anything. I'll just step away.

JANE: I wholeheartedly agree with that. Why stay with someone who makes you really unhappy, especially if you have the same effect on them? Life is too short to be a martyr. It's such a short time that we've got on this planet and it's up to *you* what you do.

I was in a relationship that I so, so wanted to work – but if it's not going to work, it's not going to work. If it's gone, it's gone. You can't make someone love you. Fortunately, there are lots of other people out there who will love you. 'Plenty more fish in't sea,' as my gran used to say. It used to annoy me when I was younger, but it's a phrase I use all the time now!

MOVING ON – THE PEOPLE WHO GET YOU THROUGH IT

JANE: When my marriage ended, I wrote a song for my mum called 'The Hand That Leads Me'. It's about how she took my hand, like she did when I was six, and said, 'We'll get through this together.' She led me through the darkest time of my life and I'll always be grateful that I had her around. Sometimes she didn't even have to say anything: she just put her hand out and touched my knee and that was enough comfort.

She also left me on my own at times, and I think that's very important too. You can't rush something like that. If you want to grieve, grieve as much as you want. If you don't want to go out, don't go out. It's your body dealing with it and your mind getting through it. It can take some people six months; it can take some people six years; and it did take me an awful long time.

ANDREA: In my experience it was two years before I felt like I wanted to carry on. Most people seem to agree that you need a minimum of two years to get over it – and that's not saying that you will get over it.

It is like a bereavement, as Jane says. You're mourning what could have been, as well as what you had at the beginning. You need time to grieve, even if you're the one who left, not the one who has been left. A lot of people make the mistake of thinking that it's all right for the one who left. It's really not.

I could not have got through my period of mourning without my friends and my family. They were really supportive and nonjudgemental of a situation that they didn't understand. I didn't necessarily tell anyone the whole story, apart from my best friend Jane. So most people didn't really understand what had happened or what was going on. It was a massive shock to all of them.

I must have bored the pants off my friends, crying and sobbing and going over and over it all again, but they just listened. I thank them for that. It made such a difference.

Gradually you find that you're crying less each time you see them and then one day you go round to your friend's and you're not crying at all. That's the moment you realise that you're finally getting better.

JACKIE: Your best friends can be a real touchstone in that way, can't they? They can help you gauge where you are in life and how you're doing.

HOW TO GET OVER IT

JANE: I feel sorry for women who think that they need to go straight back into another relationship, because that to me is doomed.

LYNDA: Yes, I always say to people when their relationship ends, 'Don't think you've got to go and find somebody else.' I'm suspicious of people who go through break-ups and waltz straight into the next relationship. You can't possibly have been with someone for sixteen or twenty years and just turn it all off. It's got to work its way through.

Everybody should be on their own for a bit, *really* on their own. Especially men, because they're very bad at it. I learned to be confident when I was on my own and it's the only way to understand what makes you tick.

JANE: I'm with you there. Being alone for a while is crucial, I think.

LYNDA: I think that's why it was such good timing for Mr Spain and me when we met. I had been on my own for ten years and he had been on his own for six years, after a divorce.

JANE: Ten years seems a heck of a long time, love, but maybe that's just how long you needed. Some people go straight back into another relationship because they need that confirmation that they're okay, whereas I tend to withdraw into

myself. I need to let myself grow again and return to the things that made me happy, instead of pleasing everybody else all the time.

When my marriage ended I got back into reading books again and going off on holiday with my mum. It was really refreshing to have a really good time without a man involved.

I really like to read; I read absolutely everything. I have quite a thirst for knowledge. I suppose that might be because I wasn't that bright at school, so I've sort of done my growing up in my thirties and my forties. Thinking that I can do anything − go back to school, anything I want − has been a revelation for me. I went to learn computers about five years ago. It was great because I really wanted to do it and I passed all my exams.

I love biographies, but I also like to read books by wise people, like the Oprah books. They've helped me a great deal and I like to get into people's minds. I wouldn't say I like a lot of self-help books, but I've got two that I go to if I'm feeling slightly out of sorts, when I've got that feeling of doom and gloom in my stomach. Sometimes just reading a chapter will make me feel better.

The two books I swear by are *The Secret* and *Excuse Me, Your Life is Waiting*, which are all about changing the vibrations around you. Since I've taken that approach to living, my life has taken a totally different path. Both books tell you in different ways to get on with your life instead of dwelling on all the things that you've lost, or how people could do this or that to you. What happens to you must be something to do with you, so change your vibration. That's exactly what I did and it was very freeing.

SHERRIE: We all buy self-help guides, don't we? I find the *Barefoot Doctor* fascinating. A lot of people say, 'Oh for god's sake, you can do it yourself!' I suppose that's how Paul McKenna has made so much money – because people need somebody to tell them what they already know. It's a therapy! That's all it is. It just so happens that I've also got volumes and volumes on psychology. It's insane, really, how many I've got. Somebody once looked at my books and said, 'What an amazing mix! You've got Frankie Howerd next to Dostoyevsky, crime thrillers and books on philosophy!'

LYNDA: I love reading too, but it was a job that saved me when my marriage to my Italian husband ended in 1996. My children were nine and thirteen at the time. Life stretched before me: these were the worst years to be bringing up children on your own, I felt.

Between 1996 and 2000, my TV series *Faith in the Future* was cancelled (even though it had won Best Comedy in 1997); Oxo finished; and I went through a divorce, which meant that everything I had was halved, indeed quartered. I had no money, I was coming up to fifty and at one point I even changed agents. So there was a moment when I had no agent, no money, no job, no husband, no nothing. I put on a lot of weight during that period.

Right, I have got to get my act together, I thought, so that by the time I get to fifty in 1998, I will be poised for the new millennium.

Having decided to do something about it, I happened to get a film in Russia, *The Romanovs*. It was one of those complete fluke jobs for someone like me, because they wanted someone like Meryl Streep, but she wouldn't go and work in Russia. So they were lucky enough to get me instead! After all, it's an easy hop from Meryl Streep to me, isn't it?

CAROL: Oh my god, you mean you're not Meryl Streep? I thought you were!

LYNDA: Precisely. Wonderful, isn't it? I was overweight by two stone, but I was playing Tsarina Alexandra, so in fact I was physically right for the part. My physical negative side was a positive.

It was the most incredible thing to be flown out to Russia to do this twelve-million-dollar film. Just to be in a country where nobody spoke English, where nobody knew me as Mrs Oxo, or thought that I was a comedy actress who couldn't do serious acting. For nine months I indulged my serious acting.

Of course, the downside to having your familiar territory taken away from you is that you can panic. I used to have terrible panics in Russia. Often I was too nervous to go down to breakfast in the hotel and I'd stay in my room. I found that admitting that I was panicking made it better. You just have to sit very quietly until it goes.

The worst thing was that my children were in England; they flew them out once a month. But it was also good in a way. I'd been with my children continually since they were little and to be without them was weird, but when I got back, I was kind of renewed. I thought, I can survive; I can do this.

SHERRIE: Of course you could!

LYNDA: Well, yes, but I see women panicking about getting older and being on their own. They're thinking, I'm never going to have a man again. The trouble with thinking that way is that it's self-fulfilling. You've got to stop and say, Okay, I'm panicking. Let's deal with the panic and move on.

I do aerobics now, which is horrible! However, physical exercise gets rid of the adrenaline that is produced by that feeling of panic. There's no question about it: if you ran around the block five times, you'd feel better. It gets rid of it all. It also helps just to own up to it and talk to other people.

I hadn't expected to find love again, but if you get your head together all by yourself, and believe in yourself, then you will attract people. I'm not saying you'll get married, but at least people will want to be in a room with you. You've also got to want to give love.

I used not to want to tempt fate, but I feel that strongly about it now that I will tempt fate and say that I got everything the third time round: the lust (and I know what to do with it); the friendship; and the sense of humour.

ANDREA: That's so lovely, Lynda. Good for you!

JANE: Third time lucky, as they say!

DEAL-BREAKERS IN A RELATIONSHIP

JANE: You've got to fancy someone. You can usually tell if there is going to be a frisson. That has to be the first thing. If there's no frisson, there's nothing. Next is laughter: they've got to make me laugh and I've got to make them laugh. It's a two-way street with me.

They've got to be very sure of who they are, and not be possessive or jealous. They can't depend on me a lot, because I'm not there a lot of the time. I'm the worst girlfriend in that way. So they have to be very sure about themselves.

CAROL: Bad body odour would probably be my deal-breaker. Don't think that would be much fun.

JACKIE: No it wouldn't! That's why I've never dated a smoker. I've never even kissed anyone who smokes. Smoking is a deal-breaker for me because I can't bear the smell. It's just off-putting. I've got a smoke detector of a nose.

You know how people say, 'I don't let people smoke in my house, but they can smoke in my garden'?

Well, I don't let them smoke in my garden. I'm a bit of an anti-smoking fascist.

California had a smoking ban for years before anyone else. This meant that if you went outside a building you would have to walk through a huge cloud of smoke because of the smokers standing there. Then there was a huge uproar when they passed a law saying that you couldn't smoke within twenty feet of the entrance of a building, but I thought it was fab! And when the smoking ban came to Britain, I loved it.

HELLO, GOODBYE

SHERRIE: Freddie the ballet dancer was my first love, but Bob Lindsay was the person I agreed to marry, when I was nineteen. My mother booked and paid for the wedding and I bought the wedding dress. But Bob stopped getting in touch three weeks before the big day – and he never contacted me again. I don't quite know why, or what happened, but we were both so young. He would only have been twenty or twenty-one – much too young to get married. I think his mother was against it, too.

I gave the dress to my cousin, who was a famous footballer, and his young fiancée wore it. Eleven years later I went to do a radio show and Bob was in the studio. 'I've sold the wedding dress,' I said without further ado, and we both laughed.

DENISE: How nice of you to laugh, Sherrie. I think I might have been tempted to punch him in the face!

ANDREA: I once took revenge on a guy by spitting in his drink. He was being just vile, really horrible, bigheaded and up himself.

I thought, I'm not going to bring you down a peg or two, because it's not worth it. But, when his back was turned, I spat in his drink, stirred it and gave it back to him. It made me feel a lot better.

'Cheers!' I said. As I watched him take a big swig, I thought, Right, I can go home now.

It was very liberating. I laughed all the way home in the back of the cab.

STARTING AFRESH

SHERRIE: I think reinventing yourself is a very important thing. That's why I move house a lot. When I broke up with my ex, I had to turn over so many blooming leaves that I had a whole tree of them going over. I don't even know my address any more, really.

CAROL: What are you running from?

SHERRIE: I don't know, Carol, you tell me.

JACKIE: Do you find that you move because you want to start afresh, but then things just stay the same, so you move again?

SHERRIE: Yes, because I'm always thinking, Maybe this will do it. Maybe this will be the change that will make the difference.

CAROL: Perhaps you're not giving it enough time, though.

SHERRIE: Maybe not, but I don't know what I'm looking for, that's the problem. I have no roots now, so I'm always looking for something and maybe I don't know what it is.

JACKIE: I understand that desire to move away geographically. I've done it quite a lot over the years. I wasn't really running away, but it was more a case of trying to find something different, going for a change of scenery to shake things up a bit. I went from the UK to San Francisco and then LA, and then I left LA for the same reason, to change, to grow. I felt quite stagnant in America towards the end, after eleven years. I like the idea of changing everything around you. It makes you nervous; it's difficult and a challenge. But it's good for the soul, especially in your youth when you are trying to figure out who you are. Sometimes you have to be away from everything familiar in order to emerge as a whole person in your own right. However, now that I feel so content with my lot in life, I think my ever-changing days are over and I want to stay put and enjoy what I have.

CAROL: I think if you want to reinvent yourself, you've got to look at more than your surroundings. It's more than just buying a new house or moving to another country. I was going to move to Paris; I really wanted to go because I needed a change of scenery. I wanted to see new things and explore a new country. To be honest, I was a little bit bored. But moving to Paris wasn't going to change me. In fact, I don't think I've changed much over the years. I certainly haven't gone through a reinvention. I might have dyed my hair blonde, but that's about it.

SHERRIE: But you've always liked yourself, haven't you?

CAROL: I do quite like myself—

SHERRIE: You love yourself, actually!

CAROL: I do! As far as I know, there isn't a law against it! Anyway, I'm not moving to Paris now because my life has been turned upside down

anyway in a very, very nice way indeed.

SHERRIE: Have you changed anything in your house?

CAROL: Actually, I am going to change my house a little bit because I'm not moving. So I might buy a new corner unit to sit on!

SHERRIE: To sit on? No, Carol, you put your cups and saucers in a corner unit!

CAROL: A corner sofa, I mean. Because I've only got a mouldy old sofa that I've had for about twelve years. I've never really done anything with my place, but since I'm not moving now, I might try and make it a bit nice.

SHERRIE: You're nesting!

JANE: Ooh, Carol, you're nesting!

CAROL: Am I? That's a bit scary!

Chapter 10

Home & Family

It's often said that home is where the housework is. Fortunately there's often a man kicking around as well, and maybe kids, or your mum, a sister, a friend, or a pet – and although all of the above tend to create even more housework, apart perhaps from the ghost, it's home and it's where we belong. Roots and family are a huge part of it. Mums are usually at the centre of things. And love is the glue that sticks us all together, when we're not at each other's throats, of course!

If you've ever looked in the mirror and seen your mother's face, or shouted at your children and heard your mother's voice, believe us, you are not alone! We're all turning into our mothers too! Here's where we talk about the people and things dearest to our heart, along with some of the most important lessons that we've learned over the years.

AT HOME

JANE: I worked on my house all last year and I've finally got a house that I just love. I walk in and it's like I can exhale. I've got all lovely things around me that I've worked damn hard for: a big telly, Sky Plus, a lovely big fireplace and a big comfy sofa. So what more do I need?

CAROL: I love staying in with my boyfriend, which for me is unbelievable. I never, ever thought I would sit in with a bloke. It just feels so weird, so alien. I'm very good at doing nothing on my own, but to do nothing with someone else always felt like too much hard work. Just having them around was uncomfortable. But it's absolutely fine with him. What a result!

JANE: I'm a bit of a tidy freak, which drives people to distraction. I'm very much a routine person; I like things to be in a certain place. I'm not OCD by any means, but I like order in my life and that can drive people mad.

I can't deal with clutter and I have to finish everything before I can relax. I can't say, 'I'll leave that until tomorrow.'

When I'm at the office, I'd rather work into the night and know that I've then got some time off to relax.

LYNDA: I'm like you, Jane. I hate mess. With Michael, it's so brilliant to live with someone who picks up a towel before I can even get to it. It's such a relief! He's not a good cook and he doesn't cook, really. That's fine with me, because I don't want a househusband. I like to be in the kitchen on my own.

When my children were growing up, I got sick of nagging, so I did the clearing up. Everybody told me I was mad, but I just couldn't bear not to. I can't be like all those parents that leave their children's rooms in a mess with things growing on their plates and what have you.

As a result, my children now can't live in a mess. So when it gets messy, they notice it and clear it up, whereas children who have lived in a constant mess wouldn't see the difference. So it has worked actually!

My mum was a farmer's wife. She worked hard all day sometimes, and I mean hard labour, but at four p.m. or four thirty p.m., you'd walk into a warm room where there was toast and jam and a cup of tea. Why would you want to go out then, after that? I truly think that if young men could come home to that it would stop a lot of trouble.

Nurturing has gone out of the window a bit, because everybody's chasing the dream and everybody's gone out to work. I know it's necessary, but to me one of the single biggest factors in the breakdown of teenage society is not having anybody to come home to. The classic thing with teenage children is that they don't want to talk to you, but if you're not there, they miss you!

I love cooking and I love creating a homely environment.

When people say that women shouldn't take on these stereotypical roles, I don't quite understand it, because I get such pleasure from seeing people sit round my table, or come home to a cup of tea and a piece of toast.

My sons say, 'Mum, will you make me breakfast?' when they're perfectly capable of making the breakfast and they've got time to make the breakfast. They're just trying it on, I suppose, but I enjoy making them breakfast.

JANE: It's the mothering instinct, isn't it? My mother still cooks as if there are about eighteen people to feed. We always say, 'When's the rugby team turning up?' I have tried so many times to say, 'There's only two of us,' or 'There's only three of us.'

'Just stop it,' she'll say. It's like talking to a brick wall, so I just don't say anything any more.

She's a bit like Mrs Doubtfire, the typical old-fashioned mum really. She can cook, she can bake and she makes everything from scratch. I'm very lucky really, because I've got this wonderful mum who is a wonderful housekeeper as well. It helps me a great deal. Her cooking is second to none and I love her shepherd's pie.

She clucks over me, but she also knows that I need my space, so she's a perfect partner to have in the house. We've each got our own little bits; she goes up to her end and I come down to my end and we just meet in the middle for meals and a chat. It's perfect, absolutely perfect.

It's funny, because I assume that everybody has the kind of relationship that I've got with my mum, and of course a lot of people don't. I think it might be because I'm the youngest. I've always been at home, really. In a way I run the family, yet I'm still the baby. They all treat me as if I'm still the baby . . . and I'm forty-five now. It's not right that, is it?

COLEEN: I'm still treated like the baby too! That will never change, even though I'm in my forties and moved out of home twenty years ago.

JANE: I've always lived with my mum. It just seems the most natural thing, even now, because I travel such a lot in my job. The one place I've just always come back to is my mum's. It's home.

COLEEN: That sense of belonging is so important, isn't it? I used to love the feeling of coming home when I was young.

JANE: Yes, and your roots never leave you and where you were brought up is always embedded in you, so I think it's vastly important to stay connected to your background and to look for someone with a shared background.

I'm so grateful for the upbringing I have had. I appreciate every single thing I've been given, and I appreciate every day when a new opportunity comes along. I think that's because I'm a miner's daughter and we lived in a two-up, two-down until eleven years ago. This success has happened to me very late in life and I'm so glad it did, because I embrace every bit of it and think, Flipping 'eck, I'm lucky! I hope people see that in me.

JACKIE: They do, Jane. It's lovely to see in you!

WORK ETHIC

JANE: My dad always said to me, 'No matter what family you're born into, you can have anything you want in life, but you've got to go out and work for it.' I always remember him saying, 'You can be anybody you want.'

He took extra shifts and my mother worked so that they could send me to piano lessons and singing lessons, both of which were expensive. They knew that I had something that was different to the others, from an early age.

I was about seven years old when I first discovered the piano. We were looking for a new house and one of the houses we looked at had a piano. As soon as I saw it, I went over and started playing it, and actually making a tune. My grandmother told my parents, 'We need to get her a piano,' and they got one off a bloke who lived up the road and was throwing his piano out. I can't thank them enough for that.

SHERRIE: That's nice, isn't it? Did they push you?

JANE: No, not in the least. They were just very supportive. In fact, I sometimes look at my dad's life and think, I wish I could have been as content as he was. Unlike him, I'm very ambitious; I've got my mother's side to blame for that. They say that you take the traits of your parents on and my parents happened to be two very different people, so I fight with myself all the time! My dad was a very content man so long as the mortgage was paid. He used to say, 'I can put my head down every night and not worry.' I'm very much that type of person as well.

My mother worked very hard. She was up at four a.m. every day to work in a newsagent's, so that she could be back to cook for my brother and my father when they got back from the mine, and for me when I came in from school.

She bought all the luxuries in life. My dad paid the mortgage, but my mother went to work so that we could have a colour telly and things like that – although we didn't have a colour telly for years.

CAROL: I have a strong work ethic. I think it comes from my mother, and not having much. I started work when I was about ten, doing a paper round. I was underage, because you had to be twelve to have a paper round at the time. I was paid eighteen shillings a week – that's ninety p.

I did it because I wanted to buy clothes; I used to order things from the catalogue and pay with my wages. So I've always known that if I want anything, I'll have to work for it. I can't stand people who choose not to work.

LYNDA: My work ethic is strong. I've told you about that casting director who told me I wouldn't get any work before I was forty, but I proved him wrong and have worked continually since I was twenty and I'm coming up to my fortieth year in the business. It's something to be proud of, I think. I've managed to bring up two children, survive a divorce and buy a house, all off the back of being an actor, which isn't bad when you consider that one per cent of actors earn over fifty thousand pounds and only three per cent are ever in work. The longest I have been out of work is six months, which is amazing for this industry, although it felt pretty rotten at the time.

CAROL: Mind you, if I won the lottery, I definitely wouldn't work. I'd do nothing, go on holiday and piss about – maybe take up a hobby. I'd always do something. Maybe I'd have more time to write, to do stuff that I don't have time to do now. I've always wanted to write and I already write a lot of stuff, just for my own pleasure.

JACKIE: We talked about this on the show and it really irritated Coleen when I said, 'If I won the lottery, none of you would ever know.'

My family would never know either. My husband and I would secretly pay off all our family's debts and mortgages. Mysterious amounts of money would appear in bank accounts. Cars would be delivered anonymously. I'd love to treat my family to all of that, but I think I'd do it very, very quietly. So every time I'm in a shop or supermarket, I buy a lottery ticket. After all, someone's got to win!

On the other hand, I'm very content with my life the way it is. It would be nice to have financial security; it would be nice not to have to worry about the mortgage. But apart from that, there's not much I would change.

THOUGHTS ON PARENTING . . .

SHERRIE: People have always accused me of spoiling Keeley. But you know what? She's turned out to be the most beautiful human being, so I must have done something right. I don't think I've spoiled her. I've just loved her beyond the point of duty. Loving someone a lot can't be wrong, and it's the same with my grandson Oliver.

My greatest joy is being with my daughter and my grandson. If I don't see them for a week, my brain turns into scrambled egg and it kills my heart, because seeing them is what I live for.

People accuse me of living my life through Keeley and Oliver. But I don't live my life through them: I live my life with them and for them. I don't interfere. When I'm not needed, I go away. But I have to see them, and that's just what I live for.

I have a good relationship with my son-in-law. I know it can be quite difficult when a mother and a daughter are as close as Keeley and I are. But it's been four years and we're getting there.

I would never just go round and knock on the door. I never go near them unless I'm invited and I never say, 'Can I come round?' The only thing I do say is, 'Can I babysit?' I'm begging to babysit all the time.

COLEEN: I bet they love that!

JACKIE: You can come round to my house anytime, Sherrie! I'm not very good at juggling home, motherhood and work. But I do my best, like every other working mum, and that will have to be good enough! You do the best you can do in all areas.

I sometimes arrive at *Loose Women* looking like death. The director will say, 'Good God, get more makeup on her!' because I look so tired and pale. I look like hell at our morning meeting, so it's down to our team if I look groomed on the programme. I sometimes think they should do a 'before' picture!

I'm usually pretty tired when I get back home from London. I feel very lucky, though. Doing *Loose Women* is a part-time job for me and I only work one and a half days a week, so the rest of the time I'm able to be at home with the kids and that's what makes me happiest of all. So I may look like the living dead, but I'm glowing on the inside!

ANDREA: I get really tired after work too, but it's unfair on kids to come home and say you're tired and grumpy, so I try to keep smiling until after they've gone to bed. Sometimes it's hard, though. One night a few months ago I was up late doing a charity event and didn't get to sleep until one thirty a.m. Then I was up at three-thirty a.m. to do *GMTV* and went on to have a long day at work. By the time I got home I was exhausted. I remember kneeling on the floor with Amy, my two year old, playing Peppa Pig Snap and laughing away, while inside I was thinking, Oh my god, I can't do this!

You have to keep smiling, but as soon as the kids go to bed the smile goes. So poor Steve gets it, bless him, although I'm not necessarily grumpy. It's almost like the Duracell batteries have been taken out of the back of the bunny. I just go dun-dun-duun-duuun duu-uun and fall asleep.

DENISE: I know that feeling so well, and young kids have way too much energy, haven't they? What's more, Louis, my youngest, is only seven, but you can't get a thing past him. I can never embellish a story when he's around, because he remembers everything word for word. 'No you didn't say that!' he'll say, before going on to repeat what was actually said.

He's girl mad. One night towards the end of summer, around nine p.m., I was in bed because I wasn't very well. Louis was still up and he said, 'Can I go and watch my favourite programme?'

'Yes,' I said, because I thought it would be like *Hannah Montana* or one of those American programmes that are on all the time.

'Have you seen what he's watching?' Tim said when he came upstairs. '*Baywatch*. Or as Louis just called it, Babewatch!'

NOT BEING A PARENT (FREEZING EGGS)

DENISE: My cousin is head of IVF at Liverpool Women's Hospital, so fertility is an area that fascinates me. He did the first-ever test-tube twins, and test-tube quads. I know of people who've had children from freezing their eggs. I don't have a problem with it at all. Each to their own, I say.

COLEEN: No, I don't agree. I'm totally into IVF and the fact that we have the technology to help a couple that desperately wants a baby, but to be able to take healthy eggs, freeze them because you 'might want them or might not, I'll let you know in the future' is ridiculous.

LYNDA: The way we're going with plastic surgery, we'll have a woman of seventy-five with a wind-tunnel face rocking a baby saying, 'Isn't it lovely?'

JANE: And that will probably be me! I got married to someone with whom I thought I was going to have a wonderful marriage and kids and everything else that comes with it, but it didn't work. I'm in my forties now – and I can't believe I've just admitted that – and it would be nice to think that there was something else for me, because it is getting a bit late for me to have children now, but I still feel very young. I also think I'd make a great mum.

LYNDA: I think you'd make a great mum too, but trust me, when they're twelve and you're seventy, you won't want to know.

THINGS YOU LEARNT FROM YOUR MOTHER

CAROL: I don't know how my mum did it, but my sisters and my brother and I have never ever had any self-esteem issues. None of us have had eating disorders or anything like that. We're all very confident. It's quite amazing. I'm sure it's the way she brought us up.

I think a lot of kids now who have self-esteem issues inherit them from their parents. Paranoid mothers who are always on diets are bound to pass their body image issues to their daughters, aren't they?

My mum was never like that. She was just normal. She never judged us; she never told us what to do and she never said I couldn't do anything, unless she couldn't afford it.

My father left when I was about three or four and my mum brought up four kids on her own. She didn't get on very well with her mother and I think she learned from that. She was determined not to instil whatever her mum had instilled in her. She wasn't a great talker, so I never really knew what it was, but I think her mother was jealous of her.

So my mum was never going to go down that road. She was just a brilliant mother. She taught us what was right and wrong, so we knew when we were doing something wrong. None of us broke the law. We never played truant from school. Okay, I was naughty: I smoked and had underage sex. But I never let her find out, because I knew she would have absolutely killed me!

She wasn't a liberal parent; she was a proper disciplinarian. She used to wallop us occasionally, but we'd learn from that.

Basically, if we did something wrong, there was no way she was going to find out. When I lost my virginity I was shit scared that she would, but it didn't stop me. I was going to do it anyway. I was a rebel.

Mostly, she let us make our own mistakes, which I think is a really good way to learn. We used to be out for ages in the park on our own and she'd never say, 'You can't go there.' That way you grow up learning how to look after yourself. I've always been very independent.

I chose not to go to grammar school, even though I passed my eleven plus. She didn't say to me, 'You're going to the grammar school!' She said, 'What school do you want to go to?'

Probably it was a big mistake and I should have gone to the grammar school, because it was the best school in Kent at the time. Instead, I went to another school that didn't have as good a reputation, because my sister was there and I wanted to go to the same school as my sister.

One of the Loose Women – and I genuinely can't remember who – was absolutely horrified when she heard this. 'How dare your mother not take that opportunity to send you to a grammar school?' she said. 'How could she just allow you to go where you wanted?'

I think that was part of my makeup. I wouldn't be the person I am today if I hadn't gone to that school. I'd be different if I'd gone and been a swot, which is what I thought you were if you went to the grammar school. I was quite clever, so I might be a boring lawyer or something now! I don't regret it. Everything happens for a reason.

DENISE: Yes, I've got a lot to be grateful to my mum for, too.

JACKIE: My mother is the kindest person I've ever met and she seems to retain that ability, no matter what the circumstances.

She's been a great mum to me and I aspire to be more like her. Now that I'm a mum, and a relatively new one, if I don't know what to do, I find myself thinking, How would my mum handle this? If I could be half of what my mum was to me I'd be happy.

I always use her as a point of reference. We're different people, so I wouldn't have exactly the same way of doing things, but if I'm stuck, I think, Oh blimey, where's the book on this? How would my mum react? What would she do?

She's very nonjudgemental; she's amazing. I can ask her advice and she'll always give me a bit of inspiration or guidance as to what to do next.

ANDREA: Everyone else thinks I'm like my dad, but I'm a lot more like my mum than I thought I was. My mum is quite quiet; my dad is the outgoing one; and, as for me, although you can't shut me up when I'm with my family and circle of friends, I'm really quiet and boring when I'm with people I don't know.

I think a lot of people probably think I'm snobby, but I'm not. I'm just quite unsure of myself, which is more like my mum. She's very confident in her own abilities, but doesn't necessarily want everyone to be looking at her. And people are so busy looking at my dad that nobody's really looking at my mum. She's the one that quietly gets stuff done and props him up.

Everybody says it and it's true: you don't really appreciate your mum until you have kids. Mum has an amazing quiet strength. I've learnt from her that you don't have to raise your voice to be heard. Sometimes the quieter you become, the louder the effect is. I'm not a shouty person anyway. If I shout the whole world stops. It doesn't happen very often.

My mum has also taught me that stillness can be a really strong quality. It's come in very handy at work.

I hosted an event up in Scotland recently. It was a big do; there were seven hundred people. Everyone was throwing the drink back and having a fabulous time, but they were getting quite rowdy and I wasn't sure what to do about it. So I did nothing. I just stood back from the lectern, went quiet, and looked at them the way my mum used to look at me for carrying on.

Everyone went, 'Oops, sorry!'

'Thank you very much, that's very nice,' I said, and I carried on. They were all as good as gold after that. I'm so glad it worked. I don't know what I would have done if it hadn't.

SHERRIE: My mother wanted me to apply for RADA at seventeen, which was very young then. She was right, though, because it was the best in the world then.

She employed a private tutor for me, so I was doing endless Poetry Society exams and LAMDA exams, apart from all the stage work, singing and dancing. But when I was accepted into RADA I was still very raw. The principal made it very clear that, although he was offering me a place, which was amazing in itself, there was a lot of hard work ahead. I didn't take that on board and messed around in the first term.

The principal told me not to waste his time or my mother's money, as she had to support me. I did realise, thank god, and started to really work. My mother was right. It was the best in the world. And I thank her for that because I wouldn't have done it without her.

ANDREA: That's a nice story! My parents were strict. They were very loving, supportive and fun, and I still get on very well with them, but there was a line you didn't cross. You were encouraged to be a good girl and I was a good girl. I still am a good girl, just a bit fuzzy now!

ARE YOU TURNING INTO YOUR MOTHER?

JANE: Yes, I've turned into my mum! I hear myself saying things like, 'Have you eaten?' and I worry about people when we're on the road: 'Get him a cup of tea!' I am quite maternal with my team and I want to look after them. So although I haven't got children, I fuss over my team. Someone said to me the other day that there are lots of ways to be a mum, and I think that's right.

My mother gives me good advice and it's always right, although I hate to admit that. She sees things from a different angle and she's a very wise lady because she's very broad-minded.

She's a genuinely nice person, whereas I've got a very quick temper and I'm not very patient.

She will say, 'Just think about the other side of this,' or, 'Now put yourself in their position,' so she always makes me look at both sides. Then I think, Oh yes, maybe I would feel a bit like that. She's very good at sorting my head out.

My mum is fine with the word 'boyfriend', but when I'm thinking of getting married, she usually steps in to say, 'Are you sure you want to do this?' She knows me so well, back to front and inside out, so she knows what's going to make me tick, and she's right every time. She can see things that I can't. I've always got the rose-tinted glasses on whereas she's definitely got full focus.

She never says, 'Don't see him,' or, 'Don't do that.' Instead she'll say, 'Are you sure you want this . . . ?' It's the way she says it that makes me think again. She's very clever that way.

It's the niggly things that get me down, and she knows that. Big things I can handle no problem. I run a company, I'm full-on and I can sing in front of thousands of people. That's not a problem. But little tiny things, like leaving a towel on the floor or nicking my chips off my plate . . . She knows that things like that will drive me mad after a while. She's very good at planting seeds that then grow on their own, until I think, Oh, I don't think I could live with this!

If we were an Indian family, I think my mother would arrange a very good marriage for me because she knows that I've got certain standards. It sounds awful, and love is a wonderful thing, but I probably would be better in that kind of set-up because you need more in a marriage and a partnership than love and lust. Although chemistry is great, it wears off. I really believe that two people should have an awful lot more in common. The sex is very far down my list. Give me a cup of tea anytime.

DENISE: I don't believe that for a minute!

JANE: As you've said before, and no doubt will again, love . . .

JACKIE: Moving swiftly on, what about you, Lynda? What did you learn from your mother?

LYNDA: My mum, God rest her soul, truly believed that if you gave people enough love, it would be returned. That's not always the case, but it's a good way to live.

My parents also taught me how to argue! On the one hand, I find it very easy to see all the sides of an argument, but on the other hand, if I lose control, I can be very cruel. I would only ever really lose my temper when I was at home, within the comfort zone of a house and a family. I realised quite early on that I could be very cruel verbally, so I try not to reach that point, because then I'm off on one and I don't think before I speak. Unfortunately, you can't take words back.

JACKIE: Your relationship with your family is unique in that way. You come from a big family, Coleen. Did you ever have rows?

COLEEN: My sisters and I always fancied the same boys when we were younger. We had very similar tastes in men. If two of you were single and a good-looking bloke walked in that you both fancied, it was a fight to the death. But once one sister got him, the other sister backed off. Going anywhere near someone else's bloke was a no-no.

Sibling rivalry has never been a major thing for me because I was the youngest, but I suppose that as you get older there's going to be a hint of it – not in a nasty, stab-your-sister-in-the-back way, but a bit of irritation, because we're all in the same position.

DENISE: There's a long gap between my sons. As my eldest was growing up, Tim and I were both very much of the 'he's only, not lonely' school of thought. If we went away, we always took another child and the house was always full of kids. He loved it, he says now, because he never had that sibling fighting. If you go away with your brother at that young age, ninety per cent of your time is going to be spent fighting, whereas with a pal that's not going to happen.

COLEEN: My sisters are like friends in a way, but it's a different closeness, partly because sisters are friends that will be there forever. I mean, if I lost a friend, I would be devastated, but if I lost a sister I'd feel like a part of me had gone with them that I would never be able to get back.

I would drop anything for my sisters. If they said, 'You've got to get here,' I'd get there. I'd go even if it meant getting fired from work. I don't think I'd jeopardise everything for a friend, but I definitely would for a sister. With a friend, I'd probably say, 'I can't at the moment, but I'll be there as soon as I can.'

DENISE: My sister Debbie and I are very close but quite different. I unfortunately inherited the party gene and the prone-to-addictive-personality gene, and Debbie inherited a Saffy from Ab Fab gene. That's not to say she doesn't love a good time: she does. But Debbie knows where to stop. She's much more in control.

COLEEN: It's funny how you can come from the same parents, but all be so different. Different looks, different personalities . . .

JANE: . . . different relationships with people. My sister hasn't got the same relationship as I've got with Mum, which is quite odd really. Maybe it's because she left home quite early and went off to get married. She was really good at marriage. She is ten years older than me and broke away very early on in her life. Perhaps that's why I stayed at home, because there was room for me at home.

My brother Tony is five years older than me. I spend a lot of time with Tony because he has a chauffeur business and works with us all the time. We always bring Tony in as the driver when we're on the road. I always like to have a member of the family with me one way or another, because I'm a very family focused person. If I could take my mother everywhere with me, I would!

SUPERNATURAL CONNECTIONS

ANDREA: Would you like to receive a message from a loved one?

JANE: I would love for my dad and my gran to come back, so that I could say thanks to them for being such a great part of my life. I really hope I'll see again all the people that I've loved and lost.

CAROL: Why didn't you say it when they were alive?

JANE: I did, but look what's happened to me in the last ten years! I want to say thanks so much for all your support in the past, and also I want them to know what I've done.

ANDREA: Do you not feel that they can see you anyway?

JANE: Yes, and I've always believed that they can.

CAROL: Well, you don't need to tell them then, do you? That's the way I see it. I don't want any messages. The only person I've really cared about who has died is my mum and there's nothing else to say. I said everything to her when she was alive and I'm sure she did to me, so that's done. Yes, I'd love her to see how well *Loose Women* is doing. She was the show's biggest fan when she was alive. But, like you say, if she can see, she can see. All right, Mum?

I believe that when people die, they die and it's done, so get over it. The point of life is that you die.

JANE: You do die, and you leave the body behind, but the soul and the spirit go on to bigger and better things, Carol.

CAROL: They don't!

JANE: They do!

ANDREA: Carol, you're very lucky in that you're a fairly pragmatic sort of person. You're quite black and white.

CAROL: Yes, I am – based on facts, not fantasy.

ANDREA: But also, you were lucky because you did say everything that you wanted to say to your mum. What would have happened if someone died and you desperately wanted to tell them something but you didn't have the chance to? Wouldn't you like the opportunity to have one last chance to say something?

CAROL: Maybe, but I don't believe you can! I don't believe you can talk to dead people. Only in films! I'm very much open to being proved wrong on this, but I know I never will be.

ANDREA: I was invited quite recently to go and see a medium and I went along with an open mind. I knew that it could be very generic stuff, like, 'Do you know someone whose name begins with a K?' 'No.' 'Do you know someone whose name begins with a R?' 'No.'

But actually, it didn't turn out to be like that at all. The person I went to see ended up telling me some really wonderful things about my grandparents. It's all a bit personal, but she told me some things that when I told them back to my mother, they made her sob with joy. She was so relieved to hear what my grandmother had to say, which was to do with the time she died, when she wasn't herself. It made my mother feel better.

So the medium told me things that no one else could have known – and the fact that I was able to make my mother feel better, made me walk away thinking, Maybe there is something in this.

LYNDA: Yes, I think there could be, and I think I'm with Jane on this. I'm sure I have got an angel looking over me, and maybe more than one.

Years ago, in like 1973 or 1974, a girlfriend called Jenny died of a brain haemorrhage very suddenly. Afterwards, I went to visit another friend's parents, who were mediums. As we walked in the room they said, 'You've brought a friend with you!'

'What do you mean?' I said, gesturing to their daughter.

'No, she's standing there,' they said, and they went on to describe my dead friend.

'But she's dead, ' I said.

'Yes, but she's there with you and she wants you to know that she will always look after you.'

So one of my angels could well be Jenny. So many things have happened to me that could have been so much worse, had I not had people looking after me. Whether I'd actually want to talk to them, I don't know.

ANDREA: It's a little bit scary, but also quite comforting at the same time. You've been regressed, haven't you, Jane? How did past life regression therapy feel?

JANE: To be quite honest, I thought, I'm making this up! It was cold in the room and the lady's voice sounded a bit funny. I thought, Okay, I don't feel as if I'm going anywhere, but I'll go with it, because I give everything a chance.

All of a sudden I was in this dream world. I could feel the heat of the place and I could smell what was going on. I thought, Am I making this up? Because you've got a subconscious and yet you're conscious and you're seeing things. The other part of your brain is saying, Is this real? So I still don't really know if it's true or not. It could just be the power of imagination.

I went back to a Middle Eastern country somewhere; my name was Zara and I ended up being taken from my family, which sort of makes sense when you think of how I am now. It made me think, Well, maybe there is something in this!  So I was taken from my family at fifteen and put into a palace to be one of many wives, but I didn't have any children, so I was sidelined. I was taken into the palace because I was a dancer, but now I'd given up my passion for dance. I had everything, all the riches a person could want, but I didn't want any of it because I wasn't fulfilled or doing what I really wanted to do. It all sounds a bit bizarre, doesn't it?

Yet, although it sounds daft, it's a fact that I've always shunned very rich men in my life, because I felt they would stop me doing what I'm doing. That has always been a part of my psyche. Then the part about never having children rings true as well, because I've just never had them. The

woman said, 'You've never had children in any of your lives.'
Blimey! I thought.

I am very much a free spirit: very artistic, independent and
financially independent. I've always been that way. When I
was growing up, the girls at school all said, 'I'm going to
marry well.' But even as a small child, I said, 'No, I'm going
to have my own money.'

COLEEN: I'm glad you found a connection, because I'm not sure
I did! I went on *Have I Been Here Before?* with Phillip Schofield
and it was interesting and good fun, but I'm kind of cynical
about all of that. To be honest, I don't know if I really was
regressed or whether I was making it up.

I was Julie or somebody-or-other, back in 1850, and when
the researchers checked out that date they actually found
three women of that name. Which shocked me, because all
the time I was lying there I was thinking, I'm making this
up! How embarrassing, I thought, because they won't find
anyone to match.

At one point I said that I was at a ball, but I couldn't
dance with anyone. 'What month is it?' I was asked.

'August,' I said.

When the researchers checked, they found that, around
then, the only time a ball was held every year was in August,
and if you were under the age of seventeen, which I said I
was, you weren't allowed to dance with men.

So it was all very interesting, but then of course my husband,
who is a massive cynic and thinks it's all shite, said, 'You
could have read a book and subconsciously remembered
something . . .'

'I haven't read a book with all of that in it,' I said.

'You might have done when you were young,' he said. 'You love romantic novels; you might have read a book and absorbed all of this and stored it up for years.'

So I don't know. It was an interesting thing to do and I am fascinated by it all, but I just want someone to prove it to me. I'm very open and I really want to believe that there's something else out there, but nobody has done anything yet that has proved it.

I've watched programmes like *Most Haunted* for the last two thousand years, and I just think it's hysterical, but they hardly ever catch anything on camera. Every time something major happens, she says, 'Unfortunately, our cameras went off at this point . . .' and you think, Oh, for Christ's sake, I've sat here for ten days and all you've produced is a load of noises off camera!

As for the noises, if I was in my dressing room with a friend and all the lights suddenly went off, we would definitely become hysterical at some point. We'd hear a million noises that we never usually noticed and even the fridge buzzing in the dark would sound supernatural. So I need to see the ghost on camera of *Most Haunted* and then I'll believe. That's why I go on watching, because I want them to prove something. I need to see something properly spooky!

Chapter 11

Let Loose – Girls' Night Out

We love a good party! It's great to let your hair down, even if it has got grey streaks in it (cleverly camouflaged, naturally!). But how far is too far to go on a night out? And will there one day come a time when we start thinking about slowing down? When we get to fifty . . . fifty-five . . . sixty . . . seventy?

Don't bank on it!

GOING OUT

JANE: I love a good girly night out and dancing to songs from the disco era, by the likes of Tavares, Chic and the Jackson Five. We all know those songs and, because they've got a beginning, middle and an end, you can put down your handbag and have a really good dance!

DENISE: I'm the same. I like to have a bit of a dance to proper pop music, songs like, 'You to Me Are Everything'. I can't bear monotonous dance music that goes on and on and on. You know – the kind where you go to the toilet and when you come back the same song is playing. It's just awful! So annoying.

So I'm always going on at the DJ: 'Have you got "You to Me Are Everything"?' Especially when he is playing that awful dance music. It's a bit embarrassing sometimes: 'Oh here's Nana, she's had a few drinks and she wants a bit of a dance.' But even the young ones get up and dance to 'You to Me . . .' Everybody likes pop tunes, every single time.

A few Saturdays ago, I was at the Press Club in Manchester, which is great fun. I was about to leave at around four o'clock the other morning, when I heard the DJ say, 'And this one's for Denise. I believe it's her favourite record . . .' Oh god! It was brilliant, and of course it meant that I stayed another two hours, until the end.

JANE: We had the best night out at your fiftieth birthday, didn't we? It was all girls and there was disco music, we had a good drink and we were dancing round our handbags. It was the best night out I've ever had!

Girls and 1970s music are the key elements to a good night out in Jane's world. That's basically it. I've realised that you don't really need men for a good night out, but a lot of women are funny that way. I think there are certain women who are women's women and certain women who prefer men's company.

ANDREA: It's all about the people: it doesn't matter where you are as long as you're with really good mates.

DENISE: I'm afraid that alcohol also plays a big part in my enjoyment of a night out, especially after going two years without it. I'm not talking about messy drunken nights, though. I just love a few glasses of champagne.

JANE: A lot of people need a drink to just take that edge off, to let themselves go a bit. Especially if we're going to dance, because we're not all brilliant, are we? Although, after a drink, we think we're Pan's People! . . . Pan's People, they were brilliant, weren't they? But when you look back now, you think, What are you doing? It always makes me laugh.

SHERRIE: I know! But they were the height of cool back then.

DENISE: They were, weren't they? I love nights where you're just with a group of friends and a takeaway. That doesn't have to be about boozing. But when I go out, I like to have a few drinks. It totally oils the wheels. I'm not saying that I didn't enjoy any of the times I went out when I wasn't drinking, but I didn't want to be out past ten o'clock at night.

LYNDA: I have to say that my tolerance levels are lower now I've given up drinking. I realise that sometimes I drank because I was bored, and now I'm just bored and I go home early. I don't miss it now, although sometimes when we go out, I think, If only I could have a glass of champagne to get me chatty! But by the time I've thought that, I've got through the introductions and we're halfway through the evening.

ANDREA: I'm a very cheap date with wine, but I could drink most people under the table with spirits. I'm very good with spirits. I can drink vodka all night, whereas wine seems to go straight to my head.

I don't drink very much or very often. When I go out people usually buy a bottle of wine and plonk it down, so I stop after one or two glasses.

Working on breakfast telly and having two children meant that I couldn't go out much in the evening because I was too tired, especially if I'd kept going throughout the day. Often I couldn't be bothered to put my face and heels on again and leave the house. I just wanted to go to bed.

I got into a bit of a rut like that. I forgot how to socialise, how to chat and make small talk, because I just did my job and went home again. Even when my girlfriends came round I'd be in my pyjamas and didn't really make any effort. But recently I've rediscovered what fun it is to go for a drink after work. People who work normal hours take it for granted that on a Friday, even if it's just for two drinks, you go out and let off steam.

I've not had that for over a decade, because I finished work when people are just arriving at their office. Who do you go for a drink with then? I was completely out of that habit. So it's been really refreshing to go for a little glass of wine after filming *Loose Women*.

Steve's got used to it now. He'll say, 'What time are you home?' Sometimes I'll say that I'm coming straight back home and other times I'll say, 'Well, I don't know.' So he'll say, 'Okay, I'll make my own dinner.' He leaves me to it and I'll stagger back at eleven p.m.

CAROL: If you feel a bit ropey in the morning, a sauna is the best cure for a hangover. It's a little bit detoxifying, I suppose. I would also recommend drinking two pints of warm water mixed with orange juice – three quarters water to one quarter orange juice. That, and a sauna, sorts me out in the morning. Food makes me feel sick, so I leave it till later.

I don't really get very bad hangovers, luckily. I know people who wake up every morning and take Nurofen, which is probably not very healthy. I try hard not to take ibuprofen or aspirin, so I'll do everything else before I resort to that.

DENISE: Alka-Seltzer does it for me!

LYNDA: I'm so glad I don't have hangovers any more! I had some killers in my time. You know, the ones when you say, 'I swear I'll never, ever drink alcohol again. Never, ever, ever . . .'

But then you have a full English breakfast, which always used to do the trick for me, and by six p.m. you're

wondering about opening that nicely chilled bottle of white wine in the fridge!

DENISE: Yes, isn't it funny how quickly you forget the hangover when it's gone?

GIVING UP

LYNDA: Whether or not it's hormonal, at a certain age, alcohol seems to react badly with women who drink a lot, or too much. It shows physically. It just doesn't have a good effect on a lot of women I know, and that was the stage I was at too. So I gave up.

Drinking too much depresses you, it makes you maudlin and it makes you fat. For me, that buzz, that lovely, slightly pissed feeling just wasn't there any more.

DENISE: I know my parents worry about me, even though they were always party people, because they know that my partying tendencies have taken me down the wrong path a few times. It started off as self-medicating for my illness, because it gave me an immediate feeling of almost normality. Then it turned into a problem because I was terrified to be without it.

Some of the time I was self-medicating, but I would never lie and say that during that time I didn't do it at a party – I did! I went down that road and it was bleak. Luckily I found my way back.

Still, for me, there's just always one more drink to have,

one more party to have. I keep thinking that one day I'll wake up and I'll be grown-up and all that will stop, but sadly it's not happening. I don't know whether it ever does.

Maybe you have to make it happen, because you're fifty. For me, there's something about that word fifty that does say you should be a bit more grown-up. Obviously I have big responsibilities with the family, so I do fulfil a grown-up role, but I still love to go out.

Should I be going on an all-nighter to the Press Club with the young 'uns at my age? I'm very lucky that I'm in an industry where there are lots of young people who all want me to go. It's not like they're saying, 'Oh no, Denise is tagging along.' In that case, I wouldn't go. No, they want me to go, so part of me thinks, Well, why not? The only real downside seems to be that it takes me longer to bounce back from an all-nighter these days.

LYNDA: Giving up the drink was a huge test of my relationship with Michael. I feel sorry for people who want to give up something and their other half doesn't – and why should they, in a way? But thank god we did it together. Well, Michael gave it up first and I soldiered on for six months.

I did have a glass at our wedding. Michael didn't, but I did. I had a glass with the toast and I sipped it. The trouble was, it wasn't like I remembered it. All I could taste was alcohol. It was a bit like when you first taste alcohol as a child.

Then I thought, Right, I'm going to taste the red wine, because the marvellous combination of red wine with cheese was the one thing I thought I would miss when I gave up drinking. But again, all I could taste was alcohol. I suppose if I'd carried on drinking and got past the alcoholic taste, it would all have come back. But neither of us are the kind of people who can have a single glass of wine, so it's better not to go there, really.

It's like when I gave up smoking: I so envied people who could have a cigarette after a meal. I can't do that. The best cigarette you ever had was after a meal, but once you took that one away, all the other cigarettes in the day were pointless!

JANE: Cigarettes are totally pointless! Especially as you don't get any real pleasure out of them, unlike a nice glass of wine. Like most people, I enjoy a drink when I go out, or when I throw a party.

I don't get a chance to throw a party very often, so when I do, it's a proper party and it goes on for hours! There's usually a band, the neighbours are all invited and my mother's still up at four in the morning doing vodka shots, long after I've gone to bed. Most of the time, she doesn't really drink. Neither of us are big drinkers; we'll have the odd glass of wine with dinner. But at a party she can down them and not even flinch, and so can I. We're made of good, strong stuff!

Chapter 12

Loose Ends

Remember your mum's odds-and-ends basket? The place where she safely stored buttons and Christmas cracker sewing kits, and how you'd always marvel at how well equipped she was to cope with anything life threw at her? (Or anything you as a stroppy teenager threw at her, impatiently waiting to go out and not caring whether your hem was uneven or not.) Well, here's our book's equivalent – the place where we safely stored all the bits and pieces that we thought might come in handy later. This is where you can read about what makes us laugh and the mottos we live by, along with life's little irritations, our favourite indulgences, what scares us and how we view technology. We also think back on some of our very first memories too, which sadly happened quite a long time ago now . . .

As we said, odds and ends: we weren't quite sure what to do with them, but we definitely wouldn't want to throw them away! And we hope that, once you've read them, you'll find one or two bits of wisdom you'd like to store away safely too.

LIFE MOTTO AND MANTRA

DENISE: My motto is: Only dull people look good in the morning.

JACKIE: That's brilliant! And very comforting too. One of the best life mottos I ever heard was from Maya Angelou: 'When somebody shows you who they are, believe them.' I wish somebody had told me that when I was a lot younger.

When you're younger and it comes to the opposite sex, you often think you can change people, or they've got potential. You're not really paying attention to the behaviour in front of you, or how the person is. You're just seeing what you're looking for and what you'd like them to be like.

Now, in all areas of my life, I judge people on what they present to me. I think that's probably a far less painful way to go through life than judging people on who you think they might be, given half a chance.

ANDREA: It's naff and it's 70s, but I've always lived by the mantra, 'Feel the fear and do it anyway.'

Also, 'If it feels right, it is right, and if it feels wrong, it is wrong.' It's really straightforward and I always use it when I meet people. If I meet someone, click with them and it feels right, then it normally is. I don't go out of my way to make it work if I don't click with someone, even if everyone else likes them. It's about trusting your instincts.

SHERRIE: Now that the break-up of my marriage and all those horrible times are behind me, I try to wake up every morning and smile and say thank you. I've got a lot to say thank you for, especially my daughter and my grandson, and I always think that if you can just smile first thing in the morning, then the rest of the day will be okay.

I'm a big worrier; I worry about everything. So I try and stop my stomach from churning by visualising Oliver and Keeley. I think to myself, Be happy! Sometimes I get cross with people, but then I think, You know what, Sherrie? Don't! Just smile, because life is so short.

The world is terrible at the moment and god only knows what's going to happen next, in America and here, but there's no point in dwelling on it. It's going to hit us anyway, so just smile and be happy and try and stay positive in your heart. My father-in-law watches twenty-four-hour news all day long and all it does is depress him. What's the point in making yourself unhappy?

DENISE: Absolutely right. I suppose another of my mottos is the old chestnut: Enjoy today because you might die tomorrow. I'm not a particularly religious person and I'm not entirely sure that there's going to be another life after this. So I'm not going to give things up in this life because of what might happen in the next. I'm still nice to people; I still do a lot for my charities; I'm still a good person, or try to be. But I can be naughty if I want to!

NIGGLES

ANDREA: I can't bear rudeness and I can't bear people who are rude. A lack of basic manners really niggles me, because it costs absolutely nothing just to smile and hold a door open for someone. You can really make their day just by doing that.

The other day I was leaving the TV studios carrying a suitcase, a bag and my coat, and a man walked through the door without holding it open for me. A female security guard saw what had happened and held the door for me. 'You're a gentleman,' I said, and we laughed.

Then another man said, 'Yeah, but I'm not!' and barged past me, literally elbowing me out of the way to get through the door. Which gained him exactly 1.5 seconds of waiting time.

Honestly, I was so angry that I could have had him by the throat up against a wall. 'You're a rude man!' I shouted after him.

COLEEN: Well done!

ANDREA: The security guard just laughed and rolled her eyes. It bothered me for the rest of the day, though. The man probably went to his desk and didn't even think about it at all afterwards, whereas I wanted to come back into the building, trace him, go up to his floor, find him and say, 'You are old enough to know better! What is the matter with you?'

I won't put up with it because the world would be such a

happier place if people were just more polite. So I'm quite feisty when it comes to rudeness: 'You wouldn't raise your children to speak that way, how dare you?' I say, and then hope they don't beat me up.

SHERRIE: Sounds annoy me. I don't have my window open in the car, because I can't bear the sound of the air. I'm quite contrary, because if I'm at home or in the car, I like to have my music quite loud. Yet I can't bear loud music if it isn't in my space.

I always think the sea is very noisy, which used to drive my husband mad, because we had a place in Spain by the sea. The sound of the waves lashing against the sand would make me say, 'God that sea is so noisy!'

'But that's the most beautiful sound in the world!' he'd say.

CAROL: You should have said, 'No, that would be the sound of you drowning in it!'

DENISE: Little things niggle me . . . the length of the advert breaks on Sky television is infuriating . . . the way people give you your change in the wrong order . . . the bits of paper that fall out of magazines . . . I find that I'm becoming intolerant of little things like that.

And I agree with Andrea, I get very irritated with rudeness and bad manners. I don't think it's all that hard to smile. I believe in treating people the way you want to be treated. Argh, I'm starting to sound like an old woman!

SHERRIE: People who park in mother and baby parking spaces when they don't have any babies!

CAROL: I understand that women with babies in the back need a bit more space, but why do they have to have the spaces right near the lift, or right near the store? They're not disabled. They can walk from over there the same way I have to.

SHERRIE: But you don't have a baby—

CAROL: I might have a baby. I just didn't bring it with me today!

ANDREA: Well, that doesn't count. If I haven't got a baby with me, I don't park in that bit.

CAROL: I bet you do!

ANDREA: I don't! I do not! I couldn't live with myself.

CAROL: Yes, I bet you do!

SHERRIE: But Andrea's got a baby at home, so she's got every right to.

CAROL: Well, then I'm going to buy a baby seat, put it in the back and then I've got every right to park in that space, then!

ANDREA: (Gasp) No! That's just as bad.

SHERRIE: I shall report you!

CAROL: (Laughs)

JANE: Can I just say that I do park in the mother and baby parking area, because there's no age limit on it, and I'm with my mother!

JACKIE: Talking of cars and parking, I really dislike ostentatious status cars, and people who feel the need to be noticed for their cars or their bling and how much everything they're wearing cost. Vulgar displays of wealth annoy me. If you're lucky enough to be rich, that's great and you're entitled to enjoy it, but don't use it to feel superior by making those less fortunate around you feel inferior or envious.

LYNDA: What annoys me is the way the moneymen all look to the eighteen to thirties age group; endless time is spent on teenagers and the young trendies. I think they've got it slightly wrong, though. I'm a baby boomer and there's supposed to be a big group of us!

My great argument with the advertising world is that, although a twenty-four-year-old advertising executive who makes car commercials with a lot of snow up his nose may well know how to sell cars to a twenty-five-year-old, most under-twenty-five-year-olds have to rely on their parents to buy a car for them. So if you patronise me and talk down to me and make commercials that I don't understand, when my son comes to me and says, 'I want that car,' I shall say, 'Oh no, that's a load of old rubbish!' However, if you appeal to me and make commercials that I'm interested in, then I'll hand over my money quite happily. Well, not completely happily, but moderately happily . . .

SHERRIE: I've remembered something else I can't bear. What's it all about when people say, 'I don't sign autographs!'? It never has worried me and it never has bothered me. I don't mind signing autographs at all, wherever I am, whatever I'm doing.

JANE: Me neither. In fact, quite the opposite. I tend to do a lot of signings after the show so that the public can come up and say hello. That's a vital part of what I do.

I used to do a lot of signings when I was in *Coronation Street*. If there was a queue that was hours and hours long and someone started telling me, 'You've got to go now,' I would always insist on staying until the very last person had their autograph. I knew that some people had been standing in that queue for more than three hours, with little children, so I wasn't going anywhere. I couldn't understand people who would walk away at that point, because that's what we do. Isn't that why people watch us?

JACKIE: I get irritated with the *Big Brother* culture of people wanting to be celebrities just for the sake of it. That obsession with fame and wanting to be famous always seems quite superficial. If you're a great actress or musician or athlete, it's only right to get recognition for your achievements. But I find the culture of celebrity for celebrity's sake tedious and inane. It gets on my wick!

WHAT/WHO MAKES YOU LAUGH?

DENISE: My children, my friends at *Waterloo Road* and Coleen make me laugh. I really appreciate funny women. I love people's stories rather than jokes about three Irishmen going into a pub, and I find sarcasm very, very funny. American humour and television also makes me laugh.

JACKIE: My kids make me laugh! The other day my little boy wasn't very well, so he wasn't feeling very boisterous and he was sitting on his dad's knee. Mickey Mouse was on and his dad said, 'Look at Mickey! Hasn't he got big ears?'

'No, Daddy. Noddy's got Big Ears. Mickey's got Minnie!'

These are the kinds of things that are so boring to everybody else but you, because they're your children.

I choose wisely the friends that I bore about my children. The ones that also have kids are much more amenable to it, but my standing joke with Carol is, 'Do you want to see pictures of my babies?'

'Aaarrggh, no!' she says. 'I'll have to pretend I think they're cute!'

If I ask Coleen advice about something child-related, or we swap cute child stories, Carol puts her hands over her ears and shouts, 'La la la la la!' She can't bear us talking about kids.

SHERRIE: My grandson makes me laugh so much!

ANDREA: My children and the Loose Women make me laugh more than anyone else.

Finlay is coming up to seven now and I love listening to his take on the world, his opinions. When he says, 'I've been thinking, Mummy . . .' it makes me all fuzzy inside. I think, Bless him!

I can remember being seven myself, so I love watching his little ideas grow. The other day he said to me, 'You know I stopped liking football? Well, that was because I got hit in the face by a football, so I decided I didn't like it any more. But then I started playing football with Jack and I've realised that just because something bad happens to you once, it doesn't mean it's going to happen to you every time. So I think I'm going to play football every lunchtime from now on.'

My child is a genius, I thought. He's figured that out at seven!! Isn't that amazing?

SIMPLE INDULGENCES

JANE: I love a cup of tea. Couldn't do without my tea. But my biggest weakness is a bag of Doritos and garlic dip.

COLEEN: I'm a complete tea freak, I have to say, but it does make life better to say or hear those words, 'Let's get the kettle on.'

CAROL: How many cups a day?

COLEEN: I honest-to-god couldn't tell you.

JACKIE: Eight?

COLEEN: More.

CAROL: But that's not good for you!

COLEEN: It is. If the phone rings, I put the kettle on. If I come in feeling tired, I put the kettle on. Whatever happens, I press the 'on' switch.

JACKIE: For me, at the end of a hard day, a nice glass of red wine and a bar of chocolate can erase a lot of damage. I'm a bit of a milk chocolate girl.

SHERRIE: I have a mania about bananas, a mad mania about bananas. I love bananas. I don't generally have a sweet tooth, but I love banana and toffee together, especially banoffee pie. I cannot walk past a banoffee pie or a lemon meringue pie if they're homemade.

But I have a phobia about walnuts. I can't bear to sit next to a walnut. I cannot stand being near one and I can't bear to touch them. If I ate a walnut, I'd be sick straight away.

CAROL: Sherrie, you really are quite strange, aren't you?

LYNDA: I love a curry, but it gives me indigestion late at night. Before I eat it, I have to agree with myself to be in pain for the rest of the night.

ANDREA: Our new bathroom is our biggest indulgence. The whole house is pretty good, actually. We've knocked down the old house and rebuilt it; I designed the inside and Steve has designed the outside.

I didn't really know what I was doing, having never done it before, but I wanted our bedroom to be like the best hotel suite in the world. I don't mean the most expensive. I was thinking about when you lie on a hotel bed and say, 'Why can't my room be like this?' Well, it can be, if you put a bit of thought into it.

I've put my foot down about very few things in the house in terms of expense, but we've got the best bath. It's like an egg cut in half, with one single tap coming out of the wall, and we've had mood lighting put in the bathroom. I can't wait to have a bath in my new bathroom! No children allowed in! I might even rent my bathroom out to girlfriends. They can arrive on my doorstep in their dressing gowns and slippers and I'll leave them a little glass of wine and a glossy magazine, saying, 'Let yourself out when you're ready.'

GETTING SCARED/BEING BRAVE

CAROL: I hate scary films and programmes. The last scary thing I watched was probably *Tales of the Unexpected* back in the 1970s.

SHERRIE: That's not scary!

CAROL: The opening titles were, weren't they?

ANDREA: The music was always a little bit eerie.

243

CAROL: Yeah, exactly! And I don't like horror films. I don't like making myself scared.

JANE: I like a good thriller.

CAROL: The other day I had to go into the basement of the flats where I live, to put the electric key in. I'd been putting it off for months, because the cellar is really, really scary. There was no light. Argh, I thought, I've got to go down there and what will I find? Rats? Spiders? It is rat-infested, I know it is.

Somehow I got a burst of inner strength and I went down there. I had my eyes closed and I felt my way along the wall. It was like something out of *I'm A Celebrity, Get Me Out Of Here!* It was so creepy.

Finally, I managed to get the key in, and instantly I rushed upstairs. When I got in my flat, I took all my clothes off and chucked them as far away from me as I could, just in case there was a big spider in my hood. It was really scary, but I was very proud of myself for going down there and doing it. It's amazing what you can achieve when you put your mind to it.

SHERRIE: Well done, Carol! I couldn't have done it myself. Are you brave, Andrea?

ANDREA: I suppose I'm quite a brave person. If it's something practical I've got to do, I just think, Right, don't be silly! The sooner you do it, the quicker it will be over with. But I can't watch scary films, even cheesy,

schmaltzy, stupid scary films where you can see the join in the makeup on the back of the head.

I don't like them so I don't watch them. But once I was on a plane with Steve, coming back from holiday, and he was watching *The Grudge*. It's absolutely hideous – it's about a lady with horrible hair and a low voice who wanders around doing evil. I didn't want to watch it, but he had it on and I could hear it through his headphones and see it out of the corner of my eye. There's this horrible growling noise that repeats throughout the film, and I kept hearing it. I had nightmares for weeks afterwards.

SHERRIE: Eeeek! Oh sorry, I thought I could feel something crawling up my leg as you said that!

JANE: You know the *Frankenstein* films, with that thudding walk that the monster had? My brother used to do that when I was upstairs in bed. He would stomp up the stairs making a horrible growling noise. I just used to get up and smack him one!

SHERRIE: I hate wardrobes. They are the most fearful thing in my life, because I saw a ghost come from behind a wardrobe once. Yes, and you know when you've got tigers under the bed? I think that's really scary too. And the dark! I'm scared of the dark!

ANDREA: Yes, but it's rational to be scared of the dark.

CAROL: Have you got a mirror on that wardrobe, Sherrie? That would explain it!

FIRST MEMORIES

SHERRIE: I was four and I was on stage, about to sing, 'You've Gotta Have Heart'. I had to take my hat off, dress off, and I had a little tap outfit underneath. You know when your mum says, 'Have you been?' Well, I hadn't.

I got on stage and saw these people looking at me. I took my hat off and weed all over the floor. I never, ever got over it! I had to tap in all the wee.

JANE: I was only little, maybe three. I was having my afternoon nap and all the laughter downstairs woke me up. I came downstairs to find that the ice-cream man had been and everybody in the family had got an ice cream apart from me. I remember crying and thinking, Why didn't they get me one? My dad gave me his, so I was all right.

ANDREA: I remember being a similar age and being lost at Edinburgh Castle. We'd all been for a family day out; looking back at photos I see that I was wearing a little kilt and a little Aran jumper. I was wandering round the gift shop when I looked round to find my mum and dad had gone. They'd noticed me notice them and they were hiding around the corner, just to see how long it would take me to realise. That was one of my earliest memories, of being abandoned by my parents!

COLEEN: I love doing that with the kids! It's so funny to watch that moment of panic. Unfortunately they always find me . . .

I remember my earliest memory so vividly – but I was only two. It was the first time I went on stage, at the ABC Theatre in Blackpool. I don't remember anything about how we got there, but I do know that it was Christmas Eve and it was a special concert for a thousand OAPs. I went on in a little yellow nightie with a teddy under my arm to sing 'Santa Claus Is Coming to Town'. As I walked on, the audience went, 'Aaaaaaah!' and it really annoyed me. Even though I was only two, I remember thinking, 'Oh, shut up!'

SHERRIE: You didn't wee, did you?

COLEEN: No, I didn't wee. I was well trained.

TECHNOLOGY – CAN/CAN'T/LOVE/HATE?

LYNDA: The Internet and downloading, iPods and iPhones – it's brilliant and we've all got to learn to do it. But, from a purely entertainment point of view, somebody over sixty would much rather sit in their living room with their fifty-inch plasma and watch a really good play or drama.

JACKIE: My husband is not really into technology, so I'm the boffin in our family, god help us! I usually know how to figure out what's wrong with the computer and reboot it, which he hasn't got a clue about.

I'm not into gadgets; I don't have to have the latest phone.

I just want it to be a phone. It doesn't have to do a song and dance.

ANDREA: I like technology more than I thought I would, although I'm not very good at it. I wish I had a cupboard in my house with a man in a white coat and glasses and a pen in his top pocket. Then I could just fling open the door and say, '*Not working!*' and he could come out and fix it. Then I'd say, 'Thank you very much,' and he'd go back into his cupboard again. No need to talk to him really. He could just come and fix my computer and go away again.

We've got most of the gadgety things in our house. However, I don't know how to work any of them properly, I still haven't found out how to work iTunes. I've had an iPod for three years; my sister's boyfriend put songs on it and I've never updated it. I'm still listening to his music because I don't know how to put something else on. But I'm up for learning. I just need a little more time.

Chapter 13

A Day In The Life Of A Loose Woman

We love being on the show and we're really proud of it, too! It's a really special part of our lives and we genuinely look forward to coming to work in the morning and having a good chat and a catch-up with our friends. So what is being a Loose Woman all about? Here's how we see it . . .

WHAT MAKES A LOOSE WOMAN?

CAROL: Integrity (I think, I hope!). Lots of things . . . You've got to be open, honest, gregarious and forthright. Otherwise you don't stand a chance.

JANE: You've got to be a certain age, because you've got to know about life, and you've got to have something to say.

JACKIE: I would say that, firstly, it's about not taking yourself too seriously. We tend to find the humour in ninety-five per cent of what we talk about, and have a laugh, quite often at our own and each other's expense.

Secondly, it's being able to talk about serious subjects and your own experiences seriously and honestly.

A Day in the Life of a Loose Woman

LYNDA: Incredible honesty is definitely a big part of the combination. What seems to happen to everybody who joins the show is that they try to self-edit initially in the meetings, but it doesn't work and then they have to give themselves to the deal. Obviously, they have to have life experiences from which to draw.

SHERRIE: The strength of the girls in *Loose Women* is the key factor, just as the strong women in *Coronation Street* make the show what it is. It's the strength of the women in the world that make the world what it is.

We've all had difficult emotional lives. We've all been on emotional roller coasters. We've had to gather ourselves again and reinvent ourselves, not work-wise but emotionally and personally. We've all had to come back from somewhere, and that gives you a lot of colour in your life.

ANDREA: Yes, we've all been hurt and we've all picked ourselves up and started again, every single one of us. We've learnt from it and we've all come back bigger, better and stronger.

SHERRIE: That's right. Not one of us feels sorry for ourselves and we don't feel badly done by. We may have been hurt, but we've all come back and said 'Up yours', and we're still here. I think that is great.

It's lucky for us that we're on a show where we can talk about the stuff that hits you in life. We can regurgitate it and get rid of it. A lot of people don't get that opportunity, but we can talk it all through.

WHY DOES *LOOSE WOMEN* WORK?

LYNDA: There's a mixture of compromise from some people and straight get-in-there from others.

ANDREA: We are the sum of many parts. We're all completely different, but we fit together like a jigsaw puzzle. It wouldn't work without all of us.

One of us is loud and opinionated, one is sexy and mumsy, one's a glamorous cruise star who is also a down-to-earth Northern girl. We've got three loud creative-actress types, three of us are mums with small children . . . and I'm the Snow White in among them!

CAROL: Enough of the Snow White business! You're as naughty as the rest of us, really!

ANDREA: I am not!

SHERRIE: *Loose Women* works partly because of all the arguments we have! And because the people watching think, 'Hey, I've been through that! I know where she's coming from.' The nicest thing of all is that we're all different ages, so we're each coming from somewhere different, even though we've had similar lives. I think that makes for a very powerful, colourful, interesting set of women.

JACKIE: We're real women, not characters off a soap opera, and people's lives change. Who knows where any of us will be a few years from now? What the viewers like is that the same stuff happens to us as happens to them.

THE PANELLISTS – ON EACH OTHER

CAROL: When I first heard Andrea was coming on the show, I thought, Jesus Christ, a weather girl! You make judgements about people, but I couldn't have been more wrong about her. She's funny and she's very, very bright.

ANDREA: I was terrified of meeting Carol because she's so feisty on the programme. But within a day of meeting her I realised that she's phenomenal. On my second day I told her, 'I was really scared to meet you, but actually you're brilliant and great.'

I'm just really jealous of her, because she says what we all think. She's a super-intelligent woman who thinks things through absolutely rationally. She's almost quite masculine in the way she can break things down without letting emotions get the better of her.

She simply speaks her mind and, okay, she might say it in a very vibrant way, but there's nothing to be afraid of. Once I got my head round that, it was great. Carol might be loud or opinionated, but she is warm and lovely with it. Don't be scared by the volume! She's an amazing woman.

CAROL: Andrea pretends to be really goody-goody, but she ain't, she's really naughty. And I like her for that. So I was completely wrong.

ANDREA: They have completely corrupted me and I'm really enjoying it! I lived a life of beige before and now they've introduced high-definition colour.

It has made me a lot naughtier. That's always been there, but I've squashed it and thought, No, nice girls don't do that. Now I realise that, actually, they do!

CAROL: I might have been wrong about Andrea, but I always knew I would get on with Coleen. I didn't really make a judgement about her when I first met her, because the minute she came on the show I felt as if I'd known her for a long time, even though I'd never met her before. I still feel like that. Perhaps because she's a Nolan, I thought she might be really retro and very old-fashioned, but she's not. She's very out there. She is just the funniest person and has the most unbelievable comic timing.

JACKIE: Your relationships with the girls off-screen dictate how the relationships go on-screen. Coleen and I do a lot of jokey banter on- and off-screen. We wind each other up and have a little dig at each other. That's the way our sense of humour works and it's what makes us close.

ANDREA: Coleen is super funny. If we're struggling to finish an item, she'll always think of something funny to say. But actually she's quite shy underneath it all. She was one of the most reserved when we first met.

Now I know her better, I can see that Coleen and I are quite similar. You wouldn't necessarily think it, because she comes across as really cheeky and cocky. But we're alike in that we don't automatically think that someone else is going to want to hear what we've got to say. We stand back a little bit.

CAROL: I knew Coleen and I would have lots to talk about, because we'd both been married to someone really famous. So I was looking forward to meeting her and having a good chat about things. We've had quite a few nights when we've both had a good old chinwag about our exes, which was good. We don't do that any more, though, because it's so long ago.

ANDREA: Coleen and I have become very close over time. Her little girl is the same age as my little boy and we're both second-time-around with our partners. Ray and Steve are really similar and we laugh at how alike they are. Steve is a man's man. He doesn't want publicity and he wouldn't come on the show. Ray is the same. He is happy to let Coleen get on with it. Both Ray and Steve won't take any nonsense and they'll bring you down a peg or two if they think you're getting too bigheaded.

SHERRIE: Coleen and I have always got on. We are great friends. I love all the girls.

DENISE: I get on great with all the girls too. I knew most of them before I started *Loose Women* anyway. I knew Coleen for years beforehand. I was with Tracy Shaw the day I met her. Tracy and I went to Blackpool to see a play that my friend wrote the book for, and Coleen and her sisters were there. 'Oh my god, it's the Nolans! I'm with the Nolans!' I said. We

didn't become close mates but we did get to know each other.

What's more, Jane and I have known each other for years. We don't know how we know each other, we just do, but we have no idea where we met.

CAROL: Jane was a tricky one to prejudge. I'd never seen *The Cruise* and I didn't really know about it, but I knew who she was because she was crossing over to become a mainstream, Saturday night, star-for-a-night presenter.

The first time I met her was when she came on the show. All I remember thinking was, How the f*** did someone who's been on a reality show get a job on Saturday night presenting a talent show?

She used to have a big reputation for being a diva – she admits that she was – so I was wary. Then she came on the show just after she'd split up with her husband and I thought she was the loveliest person. She was a bit broken at the time and she was really nice.

ANDREA: Jane has been amazing with me from Day One. She took me under her wing when I first arrived, like a mother hen. 'Come here, love, you'll be all right.'

Every time I did a link in the beginning, she'd look across at me from her seat and give me a little wink that no one else could pick up on, or a tiny thumbs-up. Just to say, You're doing all right. It wasn't done in a big fussy way and probably no one else noticed, but it really helped me.

Every now and then after a show she'd come up and give me a little pat on the arm and say, 'You're doing well, kid. You're doing all right.' She's been great.

A Day in the Life of a Loose Woman

Jane is exactly as you'd imagine. She's very forthright and speaks her mind, but she's a really gentle soul.

JACKIE: Jane is such a warm person. She has that magical quality that has made her a star – which is that everyone can relate to her because she's very normal, down to earth and she lives with her mum in Wakefield; but she has this other side to her too, which is diamonds and champagne. Carol calls her schizophrenic. It's a lovely, lovely mix.

I aspire to acquire more of Jane's focus and discipline, which I don't have. She works really hard and I admire her for how driven she is. And, as much as she enjoys her success, she never forgets where she comes from. Her mother wouldn't let her!

CAROL: Jane is so lovely, but she's a bit of a mystery, which always makes me want to get to know her better! That's part of her charisma, I suppose.

JANE: I must admit that Carol was the hardest for me to get on with because we were so alike, insomuch as we were the single ones, and yet we are totally different. I suppose that's what makes it work – the fact that we are completely different in every shape and form. Carol is wild; she's a drinker; she loves men; and I'm Mary Whitehouse at the side of her.

Carol is the one who everybody loves because she says everything that we all want to say, really. But she did frighten the bejesus out of me, I'll be honest, and she still does. Blimey what a force. So I love her and we have an understanding, Carol and I, and probably we're quite close but we're not big mates. We accept each other as we are and we've got mutual respect for each other. I think that is better than being big buddies.

JACKIE: I'm quite protective of Carol. People think she's a tough nut, when she's in fact a real softie. She's got a very good, very big heart and she's a very honest and loyal person. Sometimes, because she's a bit loud and she drinks and parties a lot, people think that's all there is to her, but she's a lot more than that.

When I was pregnant, I remember sitting in my dressing room with my huge tummy jerking, wobbling and having spasms, because the baby was kicking. 'Ahhh, let me touch your tummy, ahhh, that's lovely,' Coleen said.

And Carol said, 'That is the most vile thing I've ever seen. If you don't cover it up, I'm going to be sick!'

Both equally endearing!

CAROL: I had a thing about Jackie as well, because I remembered her as a 1980s Radio One DJ, with bad hair and bad outfits. When I heard she was coming on the show, I thought, Oh no.

All DJs are bloody boring, all of them, apart from Chris Moyles. Anyone who sits in a studio, plays records and loves the sound of their own voice is boring. But Jackie's not even slightly boring.

ANDREA: I don't know Jackie as well as the others because we work completely opposite shifts, but I think we're very similar – straightforward mums who enjoy the chance to get out of the house and speak to grown-ups.

A Day in the Life of a Loose Woman

CAROL: Jackie has this fantastically perfect humdrum life. It's sweet, it's lovely and, because of her, I have faith in meeting the right person and everything being just right. Jackie's a very fine example of that. So she wasn't a boring DJ at all.

SHERRIE: I've been doing *Loose Women* for eight years; Carol and I are the longest-reigning Loose Women. As Carol herself would say, she looked very strange back then. She had short hair and didn't wear makeup. I always thought she was quite a sharp, quick, clever girl. She has now softened, because she's got a boyfriend, but she's still got that edge.

She's very intelligent, very bright. She can overreact badly, especially about the government, but then we all can and that's why we're on the show. Carol and I have been known to spar. Not so much now, because often our views are very similar, but when we first started we were very different.

She always used to say that actresses shouldn't be on the show because it was a journalistic show. But now we get on really well. We're actually very close, especially after we did *Who Wants To Be A Millionaire* together and won seventy-five thousand pounds for charity. It was a very funny show to watch because I kept telling her off, but we worked really well together. Since then, we've become quite close. It was a bonding experience, weirdly.

CAROL: Sherrie's reputation preceded her, because she's a lunatic. She's totally nuts. She's also much brighter than she makes out.

When they said, 'Sherrie Hewson's going to join the team,'

I remember thinking, Oh good, she sounds like a right laugh. She went on about the menopause for ages, and she was very funny.

Sherrie's become a really good friend. I like all the Loose Women, but I really like Sherrie. Sometimes I think she's making up all the stupid, scatty little foibles that she's got, but she isn't.

She talks about this bloke sitting on the end of her bed, some ghost that walks out of the wardrobe. I say, 'I'm not saying you're lying, Sherrie, but I don't believe you.' We can get away with a hell of a lot with each other now. She always used to hit me while I was talking, which really used to piss me off, but she doesn't do it any more.

JACKIE: Sherrie is bonkers, and I'm sure she's always been bonkers, but there is a wisdom about Sherrie. She's been in this industry for a long time, so she's a smart cookie. As much as we all call her clinically insane to her face, and she doesn't mind, we all feel very, very protective of Sherrie. We're rooting for her to meet Mr Wonderful and have a fantastic romantic affair of the heart. She's been upset in that department and we want her to move on and find somebody who appreciates her.

ANDREA: Sherrie's fabulous! She's as mad as a box of frogs, but she's been very motherly with me as well, in quieter moments. She's a more sensitive soul than you realise.

I've a real soft spot for Sherrie. She's an actress, so she sometimes performs a little bit with all her stories, and we're all just howling as she goes off into her mad little world. However, underneath it all is an intelligent, sensitive, articulate woman, and sometimes we don't see it. She only lets us have a glimpse of it every now and then.

DENISE: Sherrie Hewson and I go back to our *Coronation Street* days, of course. She is completely bonkers and I adore her.

CAROL: My first impression of Denise was, Oh no, not another luvvie actress! But she's so not luvvie. I pretty much knew I would get on with Denise, because she's got a bit of a reputation as a party animal, just like I have. I got on really well with her when I met her and I get on really well with her now. I miss her when she's not on the show.

ANDREA: Denise is just great, probably the most fun out of everybody on the panel. You just don't know what's going to happen when you go out on a night with Denise.

She's a warm, funny, sensitive, intelligent and caring woman, as well as being naturally hilarious and entertaining. I love it when she's on the show, because you can just sit back and it turns into the Denise Welch show.

JACKIE: Denise is clearly a bit mad, very lovable and very funny. She doesn't beat about the bush and she doesn't try and hide things, which probably gets her into a bit of deep water at times. She's very straight and outspoken; you know that everything she says is completely one hundred per cent true. We're quite different people and we have very distinct concepts of relationships, but I love her to bits and she's great company.

ANDREA: Lynda is also brilliant company. It doesn't make a jot

of difference that she's stopped drinking, either. She's fiercely confident, she tells filthy jokes and she's great fun. Lynda is an institution. I think she's fabulous. She turned sixty this year and her life has completely transformed. She looks amazing, she's met this wonderful man and her career is taking off again. I've got a big birthday coming up – I'll be forty this year – and Lynda's shown me that life just goes on getting better and better. She embraces everything.

JANE: Lynda Bellingham is my best friend on *Loose Women*. We had an instant bond when we met and she's a person I go out with socially. I just like everything about her. She's class; she is someone I would like to be like. She's so respected and she's taught me a lot, even in the short space of time that I've known her. I like to learn from people and Lynda Bellingham is one I've really learned from.

She just commands respect, no matter where she is, but she's also very loving to everyone. She's very posh. She's everything I want to be, actually. She's just a great woman and she's lived. She's been through so much in her life, but she's a better person for doing everything, and she doesn't hold grudges. She's a great girl.

CAROL: When it came to Lynda, I thought, Oh god, she's so posh and she's such a luvvie that she's not going to fit in! But then she came on the show as a guest and I thought, No, she's brilliant.

And she is brilliant. I was wrong about her as well. I was

wrong about them all, except Coleen! I thought, Boring, actress, posh, no good. But she's a bad, bad woman! She's been up to such naughty stuff in her life that I wish she'd write an autobiography.

JACKIE: I love Lynda. She has fitted in so well. We're all so fond of her and so proud of her. I went to see her in *Calendar Girls* last year and she was excellent. Lynda is a very strong woman. She hasn't had the easiest time, but she's so positive. She's not bitter and she's full of vim and vigour. I hope I'm a bit like that twenty years down the line. She's a great role model.

She's very supportive of women and always has a word of encouragement. Sometimes when I arrive at work looking gaunt and knackered because of another sleepless night with the babies, she'll know without me saying a word. She'll just pat my hand and say, 'It'll get easier, promise.' She's an absolute sweetheart. I'm writing a TV drama and she's the leading lady in my head . . . I hope she likes it when she reads it and doesn't think, 'Cor, what a load of old bilge!'

LYNDA: Everybody was as I thought they would be, apart from Carol. I was a bit nervous of her. For the first couple of shows, she didn't look at me once. She never turned round to me, so I was always tapping her on the shoulder and trying to look round her. I adore her now. There's no side to Carol. She's absolutely upfront and as she is.

SHERRIE: Isn't it fantastic that we all get on so well? That's another secret of the show's success, definitely.

CAROL: Except that it's not a secret now, is it? Sherrie, you've revealed our top-secret formula and I'm afraid I'm going to have to kill you.

SHERRIE: Don't you come near me, Carol McGiffin! Aaaaaaah!

WHEN I WAS A NEW GIRL . . .

JACKIE: It was a tight group when I joined, and as time has gone on it's become a tighter and tighter knit group. Initially I did feel a little bit like the new girl, although they made every effort to make me feel welcome. It was just like any other situation: whether you're the new girl in the classroom or the new person in an office or a shop, it takes time to fit in. You have to earn your stripes and it takes a while, which is just as it should be.

CAROL: Jackie is very clever and very good at doing what she does, at controlling the debates. I was slightly worried when she first came on the show because she was a bit serious then. But this was when she'd just come back from America, before she met her husband. Now she ain't serious at all; she's hilarious.

JACKIE: I came on board as anchor quite unexpectedly and we bonded quite quickly. I was pregnant and filling in for somebody and I knew that I would be off having my baby quite soon, so I don't think I was seen as terribly ambitious, or any kind of threat. I wasn't angling for a permanent job; I was just having a lovely time with the girls! Then I was offered a position when I came back after having the baby and we forged on ahead after that.

There's nothing I love better than trying to get a good conversation going, whether it's with friends at home, or around the *Loose Women* desk.

I don't have to be too polite if someone's moaning on, because we know each other well enough to say, 'Okay, point taken – moving on . . . !'

My favourite thing in the world is to interview people. It's natural curiosity, more than anything. For me, it's far more interesting to get stories out of other people than to talk. I don't think my stories are very remarkable; they're just normal. I think what I've become good at over the past twenty years or so is creating an environment where other people feel comfortable enough to let down their defences a bit and be who they are and tell their stories without feeling anxious or interrogated. So, being the anchor on *Loose Women* is just about the most perfect job in the world for me!

ANDREA: My whole world was just a massive confusion at the time that I joined *Loose Women* in 2007. I'd just had my second baby, Amy, and gone back to work at GMTV when she was twelve weeks old. We had moved out of London to the countryside and were still in boxes; my mum and dad were staying with us, and my mum had tripped on the pavement outside our house, fallen badly and broken her shoulder, so she was in and out of hospital. All this was happening, and I went back to work.

On my very first day back, I got a call saying, 'How do you fancy having a go at *Loose Women*?'

'What? Okay,' I said.

Thinking back, that was the best way to go into it. My mind was so filled with other things that I turned up, did it, went home and thought, Right, what am I doing next? whereas if I'd had the chance to build up to it, I'd have got really worried about it.

As it was, I sat in the anchor's chair on the first day – wiping my sweaty palms on my lap, my heart thumping – and thought, Pretend you're someone else, someone who knows exactly what they're doing. This is not a problem – for someone else.

So that's what I did for the first month. As soon as the music started and the audience applauded, I pretended to be somebody else. It worked!

In terms of presenting skills, it was all fine. I can read autocue, I can cope with talkback in my ear and I can host a live programme. I never doubted I could do that side of things.

To be honest, it was dealing with the women that I felt less sure about. Normally when you interview someone, it's one-to-one. You don't usually have to take into account that there are three other people sitting there who are going to butt in, disagree and say, 'That's ridiculous!' It was a very different format to get used to.

SHERRIE: It's quite hard for someone new to come on to the show. Andrea has done well, but it took a bit of time to get warmed up. When Carol, Coleen and I are on, it can be hard to get a word in.

ANDREA: Joining *Loose Women* was like being the new girl at school. We moved around all the time when I was younger, so I'm pretty used to that feeling.

I was never in the cool gang at school, but starting the programme felt a bit as if the teacher had led me towards the cool girls in class and said, 'Here you go. These are your new friends,' and walked away. It was quite daunting, but only until they opened their mouths, because they were lovely and embracing. They were really gentle with me at the beginning, and slowly they started pushing the boundaries a little bit more.

After a couple of months, I started relaxing enough to be myself a little bit more. Since then, I've had so many people say, 'We feel like we can see the real you now.'

I am normally very good at reining myself in and reminding myself, You're at work! But sometimes you just can't help it and I've probably had the giggles three times in the past eighteen months, when I've just had to let someone else read the autocue, because I'm laughing so hard that I can't speak. Our funniest moments tend to be when it's just us. We're normally on better behaviour when guests come on: we move to one side, sit up straighter and look at them and let them speak, because it's their moment. It's when it's just us that things can go a bit wrong.

SHERRIE: We have a director who says, 'Can you let Sherrie speak?' or, 'Can you let Coleen speak – shut up!' Sometimes we listen, sometimes we don't – it depends what we're talking about. If you stop speaking, that's the end of you. So it must be quite daunting to come on as a new presenter, but all the girls have got such powerful personalities that it works, and we all bat off each other.

ANDREA: I've learned that it's important to let everyone feel like they've had their say.

Sometimes that can mean cutting across whoever's talking and say, 'Hang on a minute, let her have a say!'

Usually we agree who is going to start, and who is next after that, and after that, but sometimes that all goes out the window, if it gets really heated. I normally step back at that point, but if two of them are really going at each other, or if someone's floundering, then I'll jump in.

My role is to keep a balance. If somebody's giving far too much of one side of an argument, I'll take the opposing side, even if I agree with them. Quite often I've had to dive in and play devil's advocate. That's another thing I've had to get used to: saying something I might not necessarily agree with to balance the discussion and throw something else in.

THE CELEBRITY GUESTS

JACKIE: It was a real adrenaline surge when Joan Rivers said what she did about Russell Crowe. I didn't panic because we've got an amazing production staff taking care of things behind the scenes. They're in my ear constantly and they knew exactly what we had to do: make our apologies, and take legal advice. They are incredible at what they do; it makes my job very easy. I just have to keep my cool and follow instructions at moments like that.

CAROL: I was amazed when Dame Eileen Atkins talked about Colin Farrell trying to get off with her.

Jenny Seagrove shocked me when she said 'f***'. She was the last person I expected to swear like that. Whoever was doing the show apologised and she just carried on, whereas they literally hauled Joan Rivers off. Literally, pulled her.

JACKIE: When Jenny Seagrove swore, it just slipped out in conversation. So we made a quick apology and carried on. But Joan Rivers addressed the camera directly. There was no way we could possibly skate over it and carry on regardless.

ANDREA: Brian Blessed was a fairly shocking guest. He jumped up and down on the desk like a baboon and nearly gave me a heart attack.

Then there was Leigh Francis, the *Bo' Selecta* guy, who actually broke the desk after he came on and started doing a lap dance. He climbed up and was wiggling his bum when the whole desk crashed to the floor. He nearly fell right through it. He was facing me as it all happened and, as the desk went, I saw his life flash across his eyes like this: aaaargh! It was unfortunate that the camera didn't get it, because it was hilarious. He looked really embarrassed about it afterwards.

Leigh was probably my favourite guest. I just adore him. He's such a nice man and so charming in real life. He's got the most breathtakingly beautiful wife. When you see the two of them together, you think, How does that work? Then you speak to them and you instantly get it. She's hilarious and together they make a brilliant unit.

JACKIE: The easiest guests are the ones who know and like the show, because they know that they can't just come on, plug something and leave. Guests have to participate like a fifth member of the panel.

Obviously, we're not going to scare anybody. We want you to have a good time as a guest and we want to hear all the stories, but you've also got to give a bit of yourself. The ones who don't do as well are the ones who say, 'I don't want to talk about this; I don't want to talk about that.' But that's the show and it's what we're here for – to talk!

A Day in the Life of a Loose Woman

ANDREA: Having icons like Cilla Black, Joan Collins and the Spice Girls on the show is always very exciting.

I have a slightly different role to the other girls when we have guests and I have to think through how I'm going to structure the interviews. So I've got my 'host head' on when someone comes on, but there's still a little part that is thinking, 'Oh my god, it's Geri Halliwell! It's Mel C!' You have to be blasé about it and pretend it doesn't matter, but sometimes it really does.

JANE: One of my favourite guests was Josh Groban. Not only is he just one of the best singers in the world, but he's such a charming man and so polite, beautiful, talented and gorgeous. I tell you, if I were two years younger . . .

LYNDA: I was thrilled to meet Josh Groban, because he's such a brilliant singer. Alice Cooper was rather wonderful too. He's not at all how he seems when you look at him. I had a frisson of delight off-camera, because something came up about not drinking any more and I was able to associate myself with a real-life sex, drugs and rock-and-roll legend. 'I know, I've given it up as well,' I whispered. 'Us chaps, us baby boomers, we did it all, darling.'

JANE: Al Murray was another favourite of mine, because he's got a great sense of humour. He's a really nice guy, not at all like he is in character.

ANDREA: I loved Status Quo when they came on. They rock! They've got such a twinkle in their eyes. I often love meeting the older people who come on the show. They've been around

271

the block and it makes them such interesting characters. I just want to take them to the pub afterwards and carry on talking.

CAROL: My favourite guest was obviously Russell Brand. It was hilarious when he walked on. He wasn't even supposed to be a guest. He just happened to be in the building and the executive producer Sue persuaded him to walk on to the set. It was a total surprise. I had no idea.

In fact, I had made it my business to find out where his dressing room was so that I wouldn't bump into him. I'd spent the whole day avoiding him. You don't ever want to meet your crush, do you? You don't want to be confronted by someone you've got this massive crush on. I thought I was being really clever avoiding him.

Instead, I lay in my dressing room, fantasising about him. He's going to knock on the door in a minute, I thought. He's going to come in here and he's going to ravish me and it's going to be brilliant!

Later, I was sitting on the set talking about farting, of all things, and Denise Welch said to me, 'If you were on a date with Russell Brand, would you fart then?'

'Well no, not on the first date!' I said, just as he bloody well walked on! I could see the audience looking over and screaming. I froze. Then I looked round and thought, Oh. My. God.

He was lovely actually. He said, 'It's very nice to meet you.' He totally lived up to my expectations: his face is so beautiful; he was really clean and he smelt really nice.

He's just a massive presence, so tall and good-looking. He has the most wonderful eyes. He's still my fantasy crush, along with Danny Dyer or Gerard Butler. (Although at the moment it's my boyfriend.)

JACKIE: Yes, in her single days – not so much any more – Carol always managed to get a kiss on screen. Russell Brand snogged her, as did Gary Rhodes and Danny Dyer. I think she used the show as a prospective dating pool!

CAROL: You lot are just jealous!

THE LAST WORD

Well, that's all folks, but hope you enjoyed this tour of all the subjects closest to our hearts. We certainly did!

Love the Loose Women xx

Picture Acknowledgements

Courtesy the authors: 1. BIGPICTURESPHOTO.COM: 2, 3. Courtesy of ITV Studios Limited: 4, 5. Rex Features: 6. Rex Features/ Ken McKay: 7. Rex Features/ David Fisher: 8.

The Loose Women Childhood Photos – The Answers

Clockwise from top left: cute as a button Coleen Nolan; beach babe Andrea McLean; an adorable baby Denise Welch and finally lovely Sherrie Hewson (away with the fairies from an early age!).

LET MALTESERS® LIGHTen UP YOUR DAY WITH YOUR CHANCE TO WIN £3,000.

WIN £3,000

JUST VISIT WWW.MALTESERS.CO.UK AND ANSWER THE FOLLOWING QUESTION TO BE IN WITH A CHANCE OF WINNING.

WHAT'S IN THE MIDDLE OF MALTESERS®?

FUDGE
MARSHMALLOW
HONEYCOMB

THE LIGHTer WAY TO ENJOY™ CHOCOLATE